D1360503

IN GOD'S

HANDS

IN GOD'S HANDS

The Miraculous Story
of little Audrey Santo

by
THOMAS W. PETRISKO

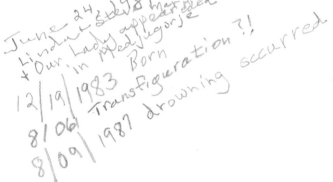

Handwritten notes:
June 24 Steve married
Linda + appeared
+ Our Lady in Medjugorje
12/19/1983 Born
8/06 Transfiguration?!
8/09/1987 drowning occurred

St. Andrew's Productions
6111 Steubenville Pike, McKees Rocks, PA
(412) 787-9735   Fax - (412) 787-5204

St. Andrew's Productions
6111 Steubenville Pike
McKeesRocks, PA   15136

Credit Card Orders Only
Toll-Free:
1-888-654-MARY (6279)

Phone:	**(412) 787-9735**
Fax:	**(412) 787-5204**

Internet:	**www.SaintAndrew.com**
E-Mail:	**order@saintandrew.com**

ISBN:	**1-891903-04-7**

PRINTED IN THE UNITED STATES OF AMERICA

CONSECRATION AND DEDICATION

This book is consecrated to the Most Holy Trinity. May God use it to help spread His infinite love and mercy.

It is dedicated to Luke John Hooker who, by the age of four, perfected the way of the Cross and received his crown of glory. May God shine light on his life so that the faithful will come to know the story of this little saint.

ABOUT THE AUTHOR

Dr. Thomas W. Petrisko is the President of the Pittsburgh Center for Peace. From 1990 to 1998, he served as editor of the Center's six Special Edition newspapers, which featured the apparitions and revelations of the Virgin Mary and were published in many millions throughout the world. He is the author of *The Fatima Prophecies-At the Doorstep of the World, For the Soul of the Family- The Story of the Apparitions of the Virgin Mary to Estela Ruiz, The Sorrow, the Sacrifice and the Triumph - The Visions, Apparitions and Prophecies of Christina Gallagher, Call of the Ages, The Prophecy of Daniel, In God's Hands, the Miraculous Story of Little Audrey Santo, Mother of The Secret, False Prophets of Today* and *The Last Crusade*.

Dr. Petrisko along with his wife Emily, have three daughters, Maria, Sarah,and Natasha, and a son, Joshua.

If you wish to have Dr. Petrisko or someone from his staff speak at your church or to your organization, you may write to:

St. Andrews Productions
6111 Steubenville Pike
McKees Rocks, PA 15136

or call (412) 787-9735

(Please submit all letters or faxes in a typed format.)

ACKNOWLEDGMENTS

This book was a gift of God in my life. I wish to thank the Santo family, especially Linda and Stephen, who were extraordinary in their charity and assistance, Fr. Emmanuel McCarthy, Fr. John Meade, Fr. George Joyce, Fr. Rene Laurentin, Joyce O'Neal, Sonia Huerta, Dan Lynch, John Clote and the Mercy Foundation, Msgr. Donato Conti, Joanne Erickson, Fr. Sylvester Catallo, Bridgette, Joe and Luke John Hooker and Come Alive Communications (editors), Deborah Fournier, Priscilla Nader and Josyp Terelya.

I am also indebted to the following people for their help or inspiration: Fr. Richard Foley, Fr. Robert Hermann, Fr. John O'Shea, Sister Agnes McCormick, Bud McFarlane, Dr. Mark Miravalle, Robert Petrisko, Dr. Frank Novasack, Jr., Carol McElwain, Joan Smith, Jim Petrilena, The Pittsburgh Center for Peace Prayer Group and volunteers, Joe and Gerry Simboli (cover design).

Special thanks to my beloved family: Mary Petrisko, my mother, my wife Emily, daughters Maria, Sarah and Natasha, son Joshua.

CONTENTS

PART I - THE QUIET HAND OF GOD

PART II - LIVING FAITH

PART III - BAPTIZED IN CHRIST

PART IV - DEAR LITTLE FRIENDS

PART V - IN THE SERVICE OF LOVE

FOREWORD

by
Mgsr. Donato Conte

I have contemplated sunrises and sunsets in different parts of the globe; I have seen immense spectacles of adverse forces of nature; I have admired artistic works, but for me the most marvelous realities of the world are the passages of God in a soul.

In your soul and in your life of crucifixion, Audrey Santo, we have seen and touched truly with our hands the passages of God, the most marvelous realities of the world. In you, immolated in a bed for years, Christ gave to us a sign, living, tangible and touching, of the love and the joy of God. Your human adventure, beautiful as a prodigy, is a wonderful page in the history of the salvation that, started by Christ on Calvary, two thousand years ago, passes through the roads of the world, crosses the city of Worcester, reaches every man and changes life.

You, Audrey Santo, are among us as Christ and you testify to us that He, He only, is the love that a young girl destroyed by sickness makes the source of life and joy for an entire people. Ask, to God for us, courage and dedication to transform our life in a complete offering and to live it and to consummate it for that Christ for whom you are suffering and you are paying in person for all. You

I

have become a woman of prayer, you are serene in your immolation, on your Golgotha, as a heroine, in a holocaust of love.

I have always believed that: the man born old, afterwards, slowly becomes young. To become young signifies, according to me, to eliminate, to eliminate always more, certain unusual things that we do when we are young; to start again. Wake up, you that sleep, and Christ shall illuminate you. Mankind of the third millennium: look at children full of life as they run; look at butterflies that dance all day and they are never tired; look at the clouds that run above you and nobody can say stop to them; look at the sunflowers, as they begin to flower even though none observes them, as they always look for sun, as they always look for God. Look around you, mankind of the third millennium, and you discover life, the vitality of life, the presence of God inside of you and outside of you.

Hear and attend to the miraculous history of the little Audrey Santo and you shall discover the mercy of God for all mankind. "The Lord has spoken something to the ear of the rose, and behold, it is open to the smile. The Lord has murmured something to the stone, and behold, it is a precious diamond in the cave. The Lord told something to the ear of the sun, and behold, the cheeks of the sun are covered by a thousand sunsets." But what has the Lord murmured to the ear of Audrey Santo? He has murmured LOVE!

Rainer M. Rilke said: "Not all things we can understand and explain, as generally we believe. The most important parts of the events are inexplicable, because they happen "in a place" where the words never can enter." Christ, Christ crucified, stop! To contemplate you, is beautiful, to adore you, that is all. In your light I am enlightened immensely. The person who passes an entire day in serene immolation, this man has lived a day as an immortal being. The person who knows life for long years in serene immolation, as the little Audrey Santo of Worcester, here is the finger of God. If only we knew how to look at life as God sees it, we would realize that nothing is secular in the world, but that everything contributes to the building of the kingdom of God. To have faith is not only to raise one's eyes to God to contemplate him; it is also to look at this world, but with Christ's eyes. If we had allowed Christ to penetrate our whole being, if we had purified ourselves, the world would no longer be an obstacle; it would be a perpetual incentive

II

to work for the Father in order that, in Christ, His kingdom might come on earth as it is in heaven. We must pray to have sufficient faith to know how to look at life. If we knew how to look at life through God's eyes, we should see it as innumerable tokens of the love of the Creator seeking the love of His creature. The Father has put us into the world, not to walk through it with lowered eyes, but to search for Him through things, events, people and Audrey Santo. Everything must reveal God to us.

In conclusion, I desire to remember the time of the year when the trees begin to open their first gems, the temperature starts to bring new perfumes, the days become longer, we are invited to live outside, and the sunsets bring a light breeze. New colors appear in nature and the season sings finally the welcome to the springtime. The things I appreciate most of the springtime are the trees: those trees that even in cities, in the gardens and in the roads, speak of springtime and of joy. Often, during my life I have observed that when the first buds are born I have admired them in their splendor open on the trees, full of lymph and life. In the early morning, the freshness of the dew of the day gives to them color and strength.

The first buds are like small children: I think they are born in the splendor of the full moon, and the apparition of the first sunshine. There joy is so much that they bring with their cry of marvel, new life to all nature. The buds are the life of the trees, like the flowers and the leaves. They are more delicate because they are the first voice of the springtime. But, I think that springtime is the season of young people, the wintertime is the season of old people, the summertime is the season of the strong, young adults and the autumn is the season of the more mature adult persons. Now is born to you a new gem. Now that God has given to us the little Audrey Santo, may we too rejoice. Be good: only a few branches are necessary to bring the springtime in our room that is full more of winter, of darkness and of incredulity. God bless the city of Worcester, all America, and the entire globe. Have pity on us Lord. Our Blessed Mother Mary protect us and prepare our hearts to give to Jesus.

Msgr. Donato Conte
Rome, Italy, July 16, 1997
Feast of the Our Lady of Mount Carmel

IV

INTRODUCTION

From Poland, Italy, Ireland and Arizona, from all over the world, thousands of people have flocked to Worcester, Massachusetts. They have journeyed to a home of the miraculous, where dozens of religious statues and pictures have wept tears of blood or shed streams of oil. They have come to see four consecrated Communion Hosts that have bled. They have come, perhaps, with the hope of receiving a miraculous cure.

But most of all, they have come to see a little girl named Audrey Santo whom God has chosen to surround with these miracles. For the life and story of little Audrey has drawn attention like none before.

The tragic victim of a drowning accident at age three, Audrey now lives confined to her bed. She is in a coma-like state known as Akinetic Mutism and receives around the clock care from a staff of nurses and family.

Yet for some reason, God has taken her life and used it in a special way. From what appears to be the Sacred Stigmata, to claims of prayers miraculously answered through Audrey's reported intercession, this silent, suffering child has become a testimony of life in a culture of death.

The story you are about to read is the powerful and moving account of the life of Audrey Santo. It is a story that will change your life for its message penetrates to the heart of mankind's very existence. In fact, Audrey's helpless yet miraculous life is a call to a world that needs to understand that either all human life is sacred or all human life is meaningless. We are either made in the image of God or we are not. Indeed, through little Audrey Santo's incredible life we are shown that not just Audrey, but the whole world is *in God's hands!*

PART I

THE QUIET HAND OF GOD

CHAPTER ONE

A FACE IN THE MOON

Most people hope to find peace in Medjugorje. Yet, it was not to be Linda Santo's experience during her first night in the remote, rural Yugoslavian hamlet. Out of nowhere, a raucous crowd formed beneath her second-story rental. A commotion started and the gathering grew. Soon after, a throng of fifty or more began to raise their voices separately and in unison, while pointing upward into the dark night sky. *"American baby's face in the moon,"* the crowd repeated in what sounded like a potpourri of broken English accents. *"American baby there! American baby's face in the moon!"*

Linda finished taking care of her daughter and hurried to the window. She quickly glanced down at the crowd and then upward at the iridescent moon illuminating the black sky.

And there it was, just like the Croatian bubbas and everyone else had exclaimed: the face of her little daughter, Audrey, was staring down at her from the glowing moon. Without a doubt, it was her child — even the outline of her hair could be discerned around her little face. "What are you doing up there?" Linda said to Audrey as she held her in her arms and pointed to the face in the moon. "Look, your face is in the moon!"

The following night, as more awe-struck cries below her window again alerted Linda, the phenomenon repeated itself. This time, however, two moons appeared in the sky, just "inches" apart! One moon again bore Audrey's face, while the other moon glowed with the face of an old nun.

The sightings were remarkable. Although unexplainable and perhaps questionable for some, these events were occurring at a place where miracles and strange phenomena have been almost commonplace since June 24, 1981, when the Mother of Christ, the Blessed Virgin Mary, reportedly first began appearing there. Not surprisingly, by 1988 this Marian pilgrimage site was well-accustomed to such bizarre supernatural reports, as pilgrims from around the world witnessed and reported on them. Many even began to expect them!

Indeed, there is no shortage of credible witnesses to these incredible events. Fifteen to twenty million people, some say even more, have visited this quasi-rustic town that is a visual and historical link between several cultures, a remnant of both the old and the new world. The pilgrims come because of the Marian apparitions and the many related phenomena. They come to pray and to find miracles of healing. They also come to personally meet the young visionaries who claim to see and speak to the the Virgin Mary.

Over the centuries, Catholic pilgrims have often journeyed to the reported apparition sites of the Virgin Mary. In fact, it is safe to say that tens of millions have done so, especially to places such as Lourdes and Fatima.

But if there is another, often hidden thread that perhaps connects many of these holy sites, it is the fact that it has been to children that Mary has so often chosen to reveal herself at these places.

The faithful have come also to understand that like such Old Testament figures as Moses, David and Joseph, who were chosen in their youth, God continues to often choose young people to be the prophets of His people.

In today's world, the celebrity of such chosen children is especially noted due to the magnitude of mass communications. For once word of Mary's apparitions and messages begins to circulate worldwide, the light which shines upon these individuals grows brighter and brighter.

Theologians for the most part conjecture that much of what is happening in the world today is a continuation of Fatima. Most of these same experts also believe that Fatima was a continuation of Lourdes. Therefore, like Bernadette Soubirous of Lourdes and the three shepherd children of Fatima, the young visionaries throughout the world today are now in elite company. Once again, for some reason, God is sending the Blessed Virgin Mary to these chosen ones with an urgent message for the world. But this message, coming at the end of the twentieth century, seems even stronger than before.

Nonetheless, the harsh reality of Mary's words sharply contrasts with the external makeup of many of her young messengers. For like the messages of Lourdes and Fatima, the seriousness of her admonitions seems to almost contrast with the joyous, youthful faces that often relay her apocalyptic warnings.

At Lourdes, fourteen-year-old Bernadette Soubirous' innocence confounded almost everyone. Her testimony, evoked repeatedly, was always perfect. Yet, the child "seemed" such an unlikely candidate for Heaven to choose as messenger of the monumental dogma proclaiming that the Virgin Mary truly was "the Immaculate Conception".

Likewise, Fatima's three shepherd children were so young and naive that they believed the Virgin Mary was referring to an older woman when she spoke of "Russia". Even Lucia Santos' mother struggled with it all. "I don't know," said Maria Rosa Santos of her visionary daughter, "it seems to me she's nothing but a fake who is leading half the world astray." [1]

Indeed, the Virgin Mary has revealed on occasion that many of God's annointed ones **"are not necessarily the best ones during our times"** that God could have picked. But, Our Lady emphasized that it didn't matter. They were **"chosen"**.

And "chosen" they had to be. When questioned, the children at Fatima also admitted that even they were puzzled at God's selection. But in their weak self-defense, the visionaries reflected no self-conceit or haughtiness in being "chosen" ; neither did they display anger or contradiction in responding to their detractors. Theologians concluded that this fact alone was all the more reason why the children were likely to be authentic. Like Bernadette Soubirous their simplicity was disarming.

Likewise, many of today's youthful visionaries have been regularly judged to be pure of heart, cheerful and normal, despite the seriousness of the events involving them. Displaying no undue nervousness or apprehension, many of them seem to be genuinely sincere, balanced and firm, like the children of Lourdes and Fatima. Most of all, they seem happy. In fact, theologians, psychologists, and medical doctors note their joy as a sign of health. The experts said that, overall, most youthful visionaries appear to be healthy, normal children that for some reason or another are "chosen" by God, just as Mary had explained.

Like the many pilgrims who journey to Marian shrines, Linda Santo did not need convincing. From what she had read, Linda believed in apparitions and such miraculous events. She believed that God was truly at work in the world, and that was the reason for her pilgrimage.

But for Linda, it was the welfare of her own child, not the apparitions or visionaries, that primarily motivated her to come to such a place and bring her daughter. For her own little girl was not healthy and happy, and she certainly was not normal.

Tragically, the glowing, radiant face in the moon was far from a true reflection of little Audrey Santo, as four-year-old Audrey was permanently suspended in a coma-like state that held no joy, no happiness and little hope for the future.

Linda Santo certainly hadn't pondered the apparent irony of it, but for some people, the reason for her trip was just another example of a world that God fills with contradictions and injustices. For if on one hand, God singles out and blesses certain youths to be His "chosen ones", why on the other hand, at the same time, do souls exist in the world who are destined for a life of hardship and suffering, such as little Audrey Santo? Indeed, in the world's eyes, Audrey is far from being a "chosen and blessed" child, like the youthful visionaries of so many of Mary's apparitions sites. Rather, she appears to be rejected and abandoned by God, destined to endure to a cruel fate for the rest of her life — a fate no child could deserve, just as none deserve to be a visionary.

4

Of course, Linda Santo never contemplated this contrasting scenario. Her faith had taught her better, and so had her mother. Indeed, Audrey's grandmother, Percilla "Pat" Nader, always believed that Audrey was special too — special from the day she was born. And although life had dealt her an unkind blow, this child still was unique and somehow set-apart.

Grandma Nader didn't just mean that Audrey was "special" because she was her little granddaughter. Like the children of Fatima and elsewhere, Grandma Nader always believed that Audrey was a "chosen" child, chosen in a "heavenly way" although in her disabled state, no one could imagine how this declaration could ever be true.

But shortly after Linda and Audrey's trip, events would reveal the validity of Grandma Nader's suspicions. For although Audrey Santo's circumstances were radically different from other "chosen ones", the quiet hand of God was at work within her in a most incredible way...

Perhaps even in a way that the world had never seen before...

CHAPTER TWO

"LIKE THE ENERGIZER BUNNY"

Grandma Nader ebulliently describes little Audrey. Like all grandparents, her grandchildren provide a constant stream of joy that flows through her daily life. Indeed, Grandparents often insist that this joy supplies a deeper sense of love and happiness even than what they had experienced with their own children.

For Grandma Nader, such happiness accrued. Ten grandchildren and seven great-grandchildren effected a ton of joy within her heart. Yet for Pat Nader (a relative by marriage to consumer advocate, Ralph Nader), the relationship with her granddaughter, Audrey, was one-in-a-million, for her little Audrey was the love of her life.

While she had been present at each of her daughter's three previous deliveries, Grandma Nader agreed to babysit on December 19, 1983, the night Audrey Marie Santo was born in Worcester, Massachusetts.

Worcester, the second largest city in New England, is situated on the Blackstone River, approximately forty miles west of Boston. Snuggled between picturesque rolling hills, pristine lakes, and numerous cultural and historical landmarks, Worcester is noted for its many manufacturing plants and educational institutions. Although its roots date back to 1673, Worcester wasn't permanently settled until 1713. It has been home to several generations of the Santo family.

Even though Grandma Nader missed Audrey's birth, once the child arrived home from the hospital, the two became inseparable. Linda recalled that Audrey let out a scream the moment she first heard her Grandmother's voice. And from then on, the relationship blossomed. As a baby, Audrey would stop crying whenever Grandma entered the room, or as soon as she landed in her arms. A bonding ensued and flourished over the years. Grandma became everything to little Audrey, and little Audrey became even more than that to her beloved Grandmother.

The relationship especially solidified due to Audrey's health. She was born with apnea, a breathing disorder, and tracheal malacia, a narrowing of the airways. Audrey's heart also presented a concern, requiring the use of a cardiac monitor until the age of three. Hospitals, specialists galore and plenty of doctor visits added up to what one might perceive as a pretty miserable childhood.

But "one" would be wrong.

Little Audrey was far from an invalid. Notwithstanding her health problems, those privileged to be around this child on a daily basis remember that Audrey was as lively as any mother could handle.

"Audrey was like the Energizer Bunny," recalled her mother, Linda. "She was so precocious, and she was fun, always fun. She liked showing off and performing. She was very verbal, and she loved to joke and tease people. She liked to say 'I'm a big girl, not a baby' and 'I'm gorgeous.' She was a real character."

Audrey displayed her bubbly personality in many ways, from parading in Daddy's boots to insisting upon retelling stories that she thought had been flawed in delivery ("Well, you just stand back now. I'll tell the story. I tell it much better!"). Quite often, the child's precocious yet lovable antics wore her family down.

First to rise, Audrey's 6:00 a.m. visits to each family member's room became the custom. Likewise, Audrey loved to sing. Her skits and songs, which varied from Sesame Street replays to passionate renditions of Elton John and Kiki Dee's *Don't Go Breaking My Heart*, habitually entertained her family. Many an evening, this three-year-old would croon long and hard for her brothers and sisters. With her little piano in hand, Audrey kept her siblings entertained with tunes ranging from the country-western ballad, *You Picked a Fine Time to Leave Me, Lucille,* to her melodramatic personal favorite, *I Haven't Got Time For the Pain* by Carly Simon.

And just as the song expressed, Audrey allowed little time for her own pain. In spite of her heart condition, it wasn't uncommon for Audrey to "rip off" her cardiac monitor. This calculated act demonstrated her feisty personality just as much as her non-stop energy. "Audrey used to deliberately pull the monitor off so we would come running", recalled Linda, "because she knew that set off the alarm."

Nor did Audrey's ailments disadvantage the rest of her childhood. In a nutshell, this three year-old behaved like any other three year-old. Tea parties, Ring Around the Rosy, riding Big Wheels, and eating steak, bacon and chocolate ice cream were par for the course. Audrey also had a fondness for quick excursions to "Mickey D's" (McDonald's), Chi Chi's and a local pizza parlor, affectionately but secretly known as "Scums".

Audrey's favorite color was pink, and she would watch *Sesame Street, Mary Poppins* and *Herbie Goes Bananas* as many times as her parents would permit her. Likewise, what would a day be for Audrey without a generous amount of time playing with her Cabbage Patch doll "Pap-patch", her cat "Noodles", her bird "Samantha", and her dog "Sting".

But for those who remember little Audrey before the fateful day which marked her painful future, they will politely vocalize that although she was a very normal child, she was also "different" — truly different.

Audrey was different in a special way. Beginning with a child-like beauty, charm and pureness that radiated from her angelic face, little Audrey Santo's sparkling blue-green eyes and auburn brown hair accentuated a look that projected pure love. Weighing only twenty-three pounds at the age of four, Audrey's presence was reminiscent of a perfect doll; one could not easily resist the desire to touch, hold, squeeze and love her. Indeed, Audrey's early pictures support and highlight these claims, and her childish aura and innocence captivated minds and hearts.

However, there are more reasons why those who knew Audrey

say that she was "special". For Audrey did things that most children her age do not know how to do.

While she printed her alphabet and numbers proficiently at a young age, Audrey had somehow learned to read before the age of four. This surprising feat startled her Grandmother, when one day, while riding down Linwood Street in Worcester, Audrey blurted out the words on the street signs.

"Audrey!" Grandma Nader exclaimed. "Where did you learn to read?"

"Grandma," replied little Audrey, "you know everybody should know how to read!"

Caught off-guard by Audrey's presumptuous response, Grandma Nader thought to herself, "Oh my God, I didn't know everybody was born reading."

They're not. But those closest to Audrey repeat that she was special— and not just because she could read when she was three years-old. She was special for many reasons, like the way she would always leave the room when disharmony erupted. And she was special in the way she always sought compassion and kindness for everyone, wanting people to "love each other" , no matter what.

Most of all, despite her young age, Audrey wanted to be close to God. She liked to go to Church. She liked to pray every day. Her mother recalled that Audrey did not pray formal prayers, she just "liked to talk to God." To Audrey, Jesus and the Blessed Mother were "all so beautiful", especially Baby Jesus. Indeed, Audrey loved her Baby Jesus, whether it was a picture or a nativity statue. Baby Jesus became Audrey's "favorite" baby.

Of course, whenever permitted, Grandma Nader will tell you about all Audrey's endearing qualities, because Audrey was her "favorite" baby. She will tell you that this child was "one in a million", the type of youngster that one couldn't help but love having around all day long. And often Grandma Nader did just that.

Likewise, Audrey fought to be with her Grandmother. Not surprisingly, since her grandparents' home was just blocks away, Audrey often slept over and would spend the day there. Indeed, the two became inseparable, like bread and butter. And as Audrey grew older, they became even closer.

But Grandma Nader asserts that it was even more than the

human tenderness, companionship and love which Audrey gave and evoked that made her special. It was more than her accelerated skills and wisdom. This child, Grandma Nader stubbornly insists, was "chosen", chosen by God before she was born.

"You know," said Pat Nader, "we knew Audrey was 'chosen'. She was a different little girl. All her life, she was a little 'chosen one' in every way. But *before* we hadn't paid attention."

Indeed, Jeri Cox, Audrey's aunt, added, "*Before,* there was always something about Audrey. She had a certain glow, a certain beauty. I mean, you would look at her, and you really didn't see her. She was very, very special."

The "*before*" of which Grandma Nader and Jeri Cox speak, actually refers to a specific event which is the real beginning of this story. For like most "chosen ones" found in Scripture and Church history, there is often a defining day, a specific moment in time which history later records as a line of demarcation in that person's life.

From St. Paul to St. Francis to St. Bernadette Soubirous, God's "chosen ones" often live mired in obscurity and commonality until a dawning day, when suddenly dramatic events unfold and God reveals His plan.

Then, it begins. God's will assumes center stage in a "chosen one's" life, and from that moment the person evolves from being one of the "many" to one of the "few". "**Many are called**," Jesus admonished His Apostles, "**but few are chosen**." Moreover, on the decisive day known only to God, the life of a "chosen one" is forever changed.

And for Audrey Marie Santo, everything began on the morning of August 9, 1987, shortly after returning home from spending the night with Grandma Nader.

10

CHAPTER THREE

"OH, MY GOD! MY BABY!"

Minutes. In a matter of minutes and in a whirlwind of activity, the lives of the Santo family were forever transformed.

It had happened out of nowhere.

Little Audrey had been playing in the front yard with her four-year-old brother, Stephen. Suddenly, when Stephen decided to step inside, she was left alone and somehow made her way to the backyard.

Then the nightmare began. In a flash, her mother went from realizing that Audrey was missing to spotting her little girl floating, face down, in the family swimming pool.

"Oh, my God!" Linda screamed, "My baby, my baby!"

This tragic accident, like all accidents, presented a trail of what later appeared to be a mixture of misfortune and irony, helplessness and destiny. "What ifs?" and "Whys?" surrounded the events leading up to that decisive moment and, indeed, well beyond it. Only God holds the answers to some of the questions. And in the end, even when all of the answers are known, only God matters.

But numerous questions emerged as part of the equation, just as they do in all tragedies. Curious, unaccountable occurrences and peculiarities which later seemed to relate to the unfortunate event in an eerie, somehow mystical fashion.

History is teeming with tales of both renowned and little-known individuals who intuitively receive foreboding dreams or signs of impending disasters. From Abraham Lincoln to the surviving passengers aboard the ill-fated Titanic ocean liner, such anecdotes often cause us to wonder what God intends when He selectively reveals some of the future in this way. Is it to help prevent the approaching calamity? Or does God offer these glimpses of upcoming trials to steady and preserve personal faith? As if in retrospect, comfort may be later found in knowing that God's presence in our lives, especially in the painful events of our lives, is eternal and vigilant.

For Audrey's mother, Linda Santo, it was no different.

The Sunday before the accident, Linda sensed that something was approaching. She sensed it in her heart and soul; an undefinable feeling gradually came over her like a fog that slowly drifts in and then silently covers everything.

Three days before the accident, Linda dreamed that she saw herself awakening from sleep. She then found herself gazing out the upstairs bathroom window which overlooked the backyard and the pool. Linda recalled seeing small children frolicking in the pool as beautiful music played in the background. The children moved around the pool in a circle. However, they were never immersed in the water. Instead, the youngsters played above it, floating like angels in a wonderland of childhood joy and carefree exhilaration.

Linda believes that the entire dream lasted only about ten minutes, and like many dreams, it had no conclusive meaning. To this day, Linda doesn't claim to understand what it meant. But she suspects that the dream was related to the impending crisis, for its mystical quality and content hinted at God's impending handiwork.

The family said that Audrey was quiet the day of the accident, uncommonly withdrawn and subdued. When she awoke that morning at Grandma Nader's, Audrey wandered outside to read the comic strips on the sun porch. Not long after, Pat Nader sat down next to her to have her morning coffee and browse the Sunday paper. Her husband, Joseph, had already departed.

Then the phone rang.

Linda wanted to pick up Audrey to take her to church and then to an outing downtown with the rest of the family. Neither

Grandma Nader nor Audrey wanted to go. After some resistance, Audrey hung up the phone and told her Grandmother, "I don't want to go. But I have to do what Mom says, I guess...you know?"

"You know you do," advised Grandma Nader. With that, the two prepared for Audrey's departure, promising to reunite for dinner.

Linda sent her daughter, sixteen-year-old Jennifer, to pick up Audrey. The entire family then went to Sunday Mass at Christ the King Church, except for Audrey's father, Stephen, who was at work at Reed's Plastics Corporation in Holden.

During this time, Audrey continued to be uncommonly silent, as if something preoccupied her mind. "When I picked her up in the morning, she was really quiet," remembered Jennifer. "And that's very unusual for Audrey. She always has something to say. That day she was particularly quiet and sat in the back seat. It was so unlike her. I kept saying, 'What's wrong? What's wrong?' "

After Mass, everyone headed to Grandpa Nader's favorite diner on Water Street in downtown Worcester. The entire family then shopped at a novelty and toy store named Rudy's.

Grandpa bought Audrey a miniature doll set and Stephen a remote control car. Minutes later, everybody headed home. It was 10:00 a.m., and the family planned to enjoy the rest of the day around the backyard pool, as they did on most Sundays during the summer. It was a hot, sunny August day with the temperature in the mid-eighties, ideal for doing nothing.

The final hour before the accident was unremarkable. The Santo family was scattered about the home, each member consumed with his own activities. Linda and her oldest son, twelve-year-old Matthew, took care of some laundry needs, since he hoped to depart for Niagara Falls at 1:00 p.m. that day. Jennifer settled upstairs to talk on the phone with a girlfriend, while Stephen and Audrey played with his new remote control car on the driveway in front of the house.

Around 11:00 a.m., Stephen entered through the side door of the house. About the same time, Jennifer came bobbing down the stairs along with Linda and Matthew. The family converged for a moment in a hallway between the dining room and the kitchen.

The "family", that is, all except for Audrey.

"Where's my baby?" asked Linda, momentarily gripped with the reflexive concern that most mothers experience countless times a day when one of their nest is suddenly missing.

"In the driveway with the toy car," replied Stephen.

Matthew jumped up and gazed out the window. Audrey wasn't there.

In a split second, both Matthew and Linda turned and dashed toward the back door which led to a twenty-foot wooden deck extending from the family room. Connected to the deck was a set of steps going down into the backyard. About ten feet separated these steps from a huge thirty-six-foot long, twenty-foot wide, four-foot deep "above ground" swimming pool. A three-foot wide walkway encased and spanned the length of the pool on both sides; while twelve-foot supplemental landing decks at both ends of the pool provided intimate contact between the water and the lounge furniture.

As Linda neared the rail of the backyard deck, her eyes focused upon the pool in horror. Indeed, her worst fears were confirmed in seconds. There at the far end of the pool floated Audrey, face down.

In what to this day seems incomprehensible to adequately explain, oldest son, Matthew, attired in his street clothes, quickly climbed up onto the deck railing and leaped directly into the pool, some eight feet away. After several frantic moments, he lifted Audrey out of the water and carried her over to Jennifer who had rushed to the side of the pool.

Jennifer, who was certified in CPR, immediately began to resuscitate Audrey. Seconds later, neighbor Mark Massey arrived to assist her. But Audrey showed no pulse or vital signs and her skin color had turned blue, indicating a lack of oxygen.

Meanwhile, a horror-stricken Linda dialed 9-1-1. She recalled telling the emergency service operator to *"come and get my baby."* Within minutes, help came. Almost out of nowhere, two ambulances, two police cruisers and a fire truck immediately arrived at the Santo home, as did a flurry of ten or more neighbors and friends, all now wanting to assist in some way. In a measure of extremely good fortune, the ambulances due to their need of repair just happened to be in the Tatnuck vicinity, where the Santo family lived.

Two Emergency Medical Technicians (EMT's), John Lynch and Michael Harris, of the Worcester City Emergency Ambulance Service rushed back to the pool and took over the CPR. After several minutes, the EMT's carried Audrey around to the front of the house where a stretcher awaited her outside the second ambulance.

By this time, however, the family's anxiety had subsided a bit. Little Audrey had responded to Jennifer's CPR and had vomited water. She was breathing! She was alive!

"Hysterical! I mean we were hysterical," recalled Linda. "It was such a trauma. We were all hysterical. The whole neighborhood was hysterical!"

After calling 9-1-1, Linda had rushed outside where a circle of people surrounded Audrey. By then, Police Officer Bourget, who heard the call on his monitor, had also arrived. His close acquaintance with the Santo family brought a comforting reassurance that everything would be all right.

Indeed, Officer Bourget took control of the situation, forcefully directing the paramedics to the rear of the house and prearranging details for the journey to the hospital. The officer also phoned Linda's husband at work, and later picked him up and brought him to the hospital.

As quickly as possible, the paramedics secured Audrey in the ambulance and departed for Worcester City Hospital. Likewise, as the family's cries of *"Please, God"* and their *"Hail Marys"* echoed over and over, they tearfully packed themselves into a police cruiser to follow Audrey's ambulance to the hospital.

While fear, shock and terror gripped them, Audrey's encouraging signs of recovery left them highly hopeful that she would be all right. Likewise, the almost instantaneous response by the paramedics, neighbors and police seemed to point to a successful outcome to the crisis.

But it wasn't to be.

Lying alone in the back of the ambulance, as no family members had received permission to be with Audrey, a second tragedy struck. Perhaps from the physical effects of the drowning, perhaps from a natural fear of being all alone, or perhaps from the overall shock, Audrey took a decisive turn for the worse.

Within minutes of being placed in the ambulance, little Audrey

Santo suffered a cardiac arrest. And suddenly, the attending paramedics were forced to administer a series of drugs in a desperate attempt to save her life.

CHAPTER FOUR

PRAYING FOR SAINTS

The motorcade to the hospital looked like a scene from a movie. By the time the caravan of vehicles departed the Santo home at 1 Rockwood Avenue, the police, responding to radio reports, had already blocked off all the primary intersecting streets along the route to Worcester City Hospital. Likewise, all traffic lights were suspended along the entire roadway.

Within approximately six minutes, the ambulance carrying Audrey arrived at the hospital emergency room. The travel time could have been better, but because Audrey continuously required CPR during the entire trip, the optimum speed remained at 35 mph.

According to the medics, the drowning had weakened and slowed Audrey's heart; they estimated that she was in the water somewhere between two and five minutes. Then, en route to the hospital, a portable heart monitor in the ambulance alerted the paramedics that Audrey's heartbeat had all but stopped.

Through radio contact with the hospital, an attending paramedic, Richard Wetherbee, responded to the directions of Dr. Richard Larson and administered the drug, Epinephrine, through an endotracheal tube which had been inserted down Audrey's windpipe in order to feed pure oxygen directly into her lungs.

As a second medic, Richard Cushing, took over the CPR, Wetherbee then inserted an intravenous needle into Audrey's jugular vein in order to administer the drug, Atropine. Together, the two

17

drugs, along with Sodium Bicarbonate, were intended to stimulate Audrey's heart.

Following procedure to the letter, the two medics also hoped that an innate reflex of the body, known as the Mammalian Diving Reflex, had taken over once Audrey's body no longer received any fresh oxygen. This reflex induces the body to automatically slow the rhythm of the heart in order to preserve the oxygen supply to the vital organs. Quite often, people suspended underwater for extended periods of time emerge miraculously well due to this primordial function that preserves the oxygen in the body.

But, by the time the ambulance arrived at the emergency room, Audrey still registered no heartbeat. Once there, her stretcher was directed into the "shock" room, where hospital staff took over her care.

Meanwhile, as the police cruiser with the Santo family pulled up to the hospital, the family's spirits unexpectedly received another positive boost.

Jennifer noticed Dr. Riordan, their family pediatrician, exiting the hospital chapel. Within seconds, the doctor jumped into the police car and journeyed the remaining way to the emergency room with the family. It was an incredible stroke of good fortune, just like the instant availability of the ambulances. All in all, the family couldn't help but hope that this was another indication that everything would be okay.

But as the medical attention for Audrey shifted into high gear, the Santo family was forced to sit and wait. The hospital did not permit family members to be with Audrey because of the nature of the emergency. Therefore, the shock and anguish of the accident began to settle in on them.

Still, Dr. Riordan's presence continued to be a blessing, especially for Linda, for it gave her a needed boost of confidence in the medical care that Audrey was receiving. Indeed, although the Santo family was in the grip of a crisis, it was déjá vu for the family pediatrician, who over the years had shared in many of the family's ups and downs involving serious medical emergencies.

And there had been a mountain of them.

With great candor, Linda Santo openly reveals that although

she attended Mass almost daily throughout her life, and certainly was a person who knew and practiced the power of faith, her prayers were never directed toward her children's physical health.

Rather, from the moment Linda became pregnant with each of her children, she would always beseech Heaven on behalf of their souls. And if God would be so inclined, Linda reminded Him that she would like to have a saint.

Linda Lorraine Nader, the youngest of three sisters, had been under spiritual direction since the age of nine. She entered a cloistered Carmelite Order in Roxbury, Massachusetts, at the age of fifteen. After becoming seriously ill from sleeping on the hay at the convent, she discontinued her efforts to become a nun.

But instead of terminating her life of faith; Linda continued to practice it at a profound level. Her parents, Joseph and Percilla Nader, were both Catholics. They both attended Mass almost on a daily basis. The Friday night family Rosary was a must. Linda's Lebanese father belonged to the Maronite Rite, an Eastern Catholic Church. The Maronite rite has a history reaching back to the fifth century. Its patriarch resides in Beirut but has jurisdiction over dioceses in Lebanon, Syria, Egypt, Australia, Brazil and the United States. Linda's mother came from French and Spanish roots and was Roman Catholic.

Thus, with such a rich spiritual background, praying for a saint with each pregnancy was quite logical for Linda, as her immediate attention always focused upon the salvation of her children's souls.

"Every time I got pregnant, I would call my spiritual director so that he would pray for me," said Linda. "Then we would meet at church so that he could consecrate the babies to the Immaculate Heart of Mary and the Sacred Heart of Jesus. Afterward, I'd say, 'You know what to pray for, Father,' and he'd always say, *'Pray for a saint!'* "

Indeed, that's exactly what Linda would pray for — a little saint. In turn, with hope and confidence that God would grant her prayers, Linda never prayed on behalf of her children's health.

"I figured that the salvation of their souls was a little more important than their physical health," said Linda, "I could give them life...but I couldn't give them eternal life."

It was a heroic prayer because Linda Santo was deliberately

concentrating on her children's souls and not on their earthly needs. And for some unknown reasons, Linda's children were not strangers to life's twists and turns and ups and downs. Indeed, her children's health, or lack of it, was always at the forefront of their lives.

This was where Dr. Riordan, the Santo's life-long pediatrician, comes in, as he was somewhat of a permanent family fixture. For starting with her oldest, Jennifer, to her youngest, Audrey, Linda's children experienced a litany of health emergencies which regularly involved the good doctor.

Jennifer had virtually lived in and out of hospitals and was bedridden until almost six years old. The child endured open-heart, kidney and bladder surgery, along with a host of lesser ailments. On one occasion, at the age of four, Jennifer suffered a cardiac arrest. Linda's oldest son, Matthew, suffered cardiac and respiratory arrest four times before he was ten months old because of heart problems. And the youngest son, Stephen, continues until this day to struggle with a form of heart disease that will eventually require replacement of his main heart valve.

Like most families, a string of lesser disorders, illnesses, accidents and ailments also plagued the kids over the years. Thus, Dr. Riordan's August afternoon rendezvous with the Santo family was far from rare.

But this time, despite the family's embattled yet triumphant health history, the situation seemed more serious.

And it was.

In fact, by 1:00 p.m. that afternoon, Audrey's life continued to hang in the balance. Linda recalled that although Dr. Riordan reported to the family that "the doctors have given Audrey some medicine, her heart is beating and everything is going to be 'okay'," this was not the case.

Within a short time, Linda's sister, Jeri, arrived at Worcester City Hospital, and along with Linda and Jennifer, the three prayed together and begged God for Audrey's life.

Words, it must be noted, could not describe the tension of the situation, as the stress grew so overwhelming that both Linda and Jennifer repeatedly found themselves in the hospital bathroom uncontrollably shaking and vomiting.

"It was a nightmare," said Jennifer recalling her thoughts from the time she first administered CPR to Audrey to the ordeal at the hospital. "All I kept thinking was 'Audrey, breathe. Audrey, open your eyes.' It was like a movie. It was so unbelievable."

Then, a little after 1:00 p.m., Dr. Riordan brought some discomforting news. Audrey was in stable, but critical, condition. And although a chest X-ray of her lungs and heart proved normal, she would still need to be immediately transferred to a hospital better equipped to handle her needs.

Shortly after Dr. Riordan's announcement, a second motorcade of vehicles sped off to the University of Massachusetts Medical Center, some ten miles away, where again another turn of events transpired that would further alter little Audrey Santo's life.

This time, however, it would be in a way in which she would never again be the same.

CHAPTER FIVE

IN GOD'S HANDS

When she arrived at her daughter's house with some fresh fruit and vegetables for dinner, Grandma Nader couldn't believe her ears. As she slowly listened to the neighbors explain how her beloved, cherished granddaughter Audrey had fallen into the swimming pool, she became overwhelmed with fear and grief. Indeed, her crushing anguish became almost unbearable, but like everyone else, when she heard about Audrey's encouraging signs of recovery, she clung to some hope.

But shortly after her arrival at the Trauma Unit of the University of Massachusetts Medical Center, Pat Nader realized that the situation was very serious.

It must have been. Once more, Audrey's escort from Worcester City Hospital to the University of Massachusetts Medical Center involved a full regatta of busy emergency vehicles. As previously, the transfer route required careful insulation of traffic to ensure her swift and safe arrival. Intersecting streets were roadblocked. And for extra protection, the caravan of vehicles received a police motorcycle escort to the east side facility.

Once again, no member of the Santo family rode with Audrey in the ambulance. However, her pediatrician, Dr. Riordan, received permission to accompany her. But this was probably the last comforting event to occur for the Santo family, and according to Linda, everything went downhill from then on.

At the University of Massachusetts Medical Center, the awaiting physicians quickly ushered Audrey into the back of the emergency room. Then at 2:40 p.m., the doctors moved her to the pediatric intensive care unit (PICU). But once there, the hospital barred Dr. Riordan from attending due to his lack of staff privileges at the center.

The physicians treating Audrey at the University of Massachusetts Medical Center extubated and reintubated her, even though the X-rays taken at Worcester City Hospital had revealed that the endotracheal tube was in *"good position"*. Unfortunately, the new tubing proved to be too large, as did the catheter; which produced a prolapse and subsequently caused bleeding.

Then, a most significant and critical event occurred. Following a preestablished procedure for such cases, the doctors injected Audrey with a powerful, paralyzing drug named Pavulon. As Pauvlon is a strong narcotic, it deliberately introduces unconsciousness. In most cases, doctors administer the drug in order to be able to work on patients without any worry of resistance from them. However, the suggested dosage of this drug differs for children and adults, and many hospitals even refuse to use it with children, preferring to give them Valium. Audrey received Pavulon for the rest of the day and for the next forty-eight hours.

By evening, the Santo family no longer received any optimistic news. Audrey had not regained consciousness. And to make matters worse, the hospital held a press conference without first consulting the family, which further exacerbated their agony.

The accident drew intense media attention that day, and the hospital felt the need to respond. But it did so in a most surprising manner. To the astonishment of the Santo family, a pediatric resident told the assembled journalists and television personnel what she felt needed to be emphasized.

"This is what happens," the resident said, "when parents don't watch their children around the pool." Then moments later, the young doctor marched into the family waiting room and delivered her prognosis to the Santos: *"Audrey is going to die."*

The family was stunned!

"They said she had severe brain damage and wasn't going to make it," recalled Linda. "She also possibly had heart damage from the cardiac arrest. They gave her twenty-four to forty-eight hours to live."

Several days later, Audrey had already proven the doctors wrong, as she miraculously clung to life.

The doctors then began to administer a series of powerful depressants, including Phenobarbitol, in a deliberate effort to induce a "chemical brain" coma. According to experts, the theoretical basis of this treatment regime is an attempt to "freeze" the brain. This hopefully allows the brain to recover from the "lack of oxygen" insult it has undergone, which is always the primary concern in a drowning. However, some experts recommend this approach only if it is administered immediately at the drowning site. This obviously wasn't the case with Audrey.

Everything considered, the family believed that the drugs and their questionable dosages may have incapacitated Audrey's ability to breathe on her own, thereby perhaps resulting in the necessity of a ventilator to sustain her life. Hospital records at Worcester City Hospital reveal that at 1:06 p.m. on August 9th, Audrey was breathing on her own.

Though horrified and aghast, the bitter prognosis did not cause the family's faith to waver. Linda, her husband, Stephen, and Grandma Nader, together with the rest of the family, became of one mind-set: *Audrey was not going to die!* They were soon joined in a constant vigil of prayer at the hospital by literally hundreds of friends and relatives.

"I didn't know what was going to happen," said Linda, "but we knew she wasn't going to die. We prayed and prayed and prayed. We just knew Audrey wasn't going to die!"

After one week, Audrey was moved to an isolation ward because of the excessive visitations, but the doctors' grim prognosis remained the same. Audrey was not going to make it. Regardless of the family's stubborn faith, the doctors maintained their death watch.

"I never believe a doctor's prognosis unless he walks on water," said Linda. "We still believed Audrey was not going to die."

Indeed, in light of all the near-death emergencies this mother had previously faced with her other three children, Linda Santo had every right to maintain such a bold and definitive position.

Besides, Linda insisted, it was already apparent to her what was going on: *Audrey was in God's hands!*

CHAPTER SIX

THE "IMPOSSIBLE"

Forty-eight hours passed, and Audrey did not die. Likewise, forty-eight days passed, and still the three-year-old clung to life. But while she did not die, neither did Audrey recover. Her family literally lived in the hospital day and night for the first several weeks, and her doctors adhered to their prognosis.

A surgical procedure called a "fundoplication" was performed so that Audrey would not vomit or aspirate. But that was it. Besides the drug therapy, nothing else significant was attempted.

Before long, days turned into weeks and weeks into months. Still the family heard nothing new. After two months, the doctors' conclusion essentially remained the same: Audrey had experienced permanent heart, lung and brain damage and could not be expected to survive. She should be "removed" from life support.

The media reported that Audrey now lived in a coma, but their information was incorrect. After several days, Audrey had opened her eyes. Although unresponsive to direct communication, the fact that she opened her eyes meant that Audrey could not be labeled comatose.

From their evaluations and consultations, the hospital informed the family that Audrey's condition was so rare that there existed no specialists in this field. But Linda refused to believe this. She managed to locate two doctors who held expertise in such cases, one in

Ann Arbor, Michigan, and the other in San Francisco. These physicians diagnosed Audrey Santo as having Akinetic Mutism.

According to *Taber's Cyclopedic Medical Dictionary,* Akinetic Mutism is a syndrome that consists of mutism (inability to speak, often seen in severe forms of mental disorder) along with the loss of physical movement and the apparent loss of feeling.

In little Audrey this condition manifested itself in a unique way. For although Audrey received an insult to the brain, she never experienced any seizures. Therefore, her condition differed from classical cases of Akinetic Mutism.

In addition, it is important to note that Audrey's condition also differed from a "vegetative state", in that all of her vital organs continued to function perfectly. Unlike the usual person in such a state, Audrey's brain still directed her bodily operations normally. This meant that her hair, nails and skin grew and functioned as usual, with no change at all.

All together, the characteristics of Audrey's condition seemed to reflect various clinical states of known "brain trauma"; at the same time, she exhibited characteristics that were markedly different.

Once more, Audrey Santo was proving to be special in an undefinable way!

While Audrey showed no significant change, the ordeal for the Santo family did change. They now entered a new phase, a stage of fighting depression while trying to maintain hope.

As the weeks crawled by, the medical team attending Audrey not only offered no hope, but also provided very few answers to the family's questions. To compound matters, repeated family requests to move Audrey to another health facility were constantly met with responses that left them feeling "fearful" to attempt anything new.

The hospital repeatedly maintained that such an action was *impossible* and would "kill" little Audrey. Their position at the time was adamant: The family should not even think of moving Audrey.

While each family member struggled in his or her own way to cope with the crisis, Linda Santo found herself in the most difficult position of all. For just five weeks after the accident, her husband left her. The entire ordeal proved too much for Stephen Santo, and he couldn't cope with it any longer. His guilt over the accident, along with an alcohol problem, caused him to seek a separation.

Thus, at thirty-four years of age, with no husband, and four children each of whom presented serious health concerns, Linda Santo found herself in the "make or break" situation of her life. It was a situation many believed to be *impossible* for a mere "housewife". But Linda prayed to God for strength and slowly went forward.

The hospital phase of the ordeal lasted four months — four long, painful and grueling months. Each day, the family stayed with Audrey, hoping and praying that she would come out of the coma-like state. Most of all, no one could bear to see her left alone.

"The months we had Audrey in the hospital were heartbreaking," recalled Grandma Nader. "I couldn't leave that hospital. The only time I would leave was to go home and take a bath. The family was always there. We felt we had to be with Audrey."

While spending her days with Audrey at the hospital, Grandma Nader's evenings were just as demanding. After the accident occurred, she especially took it upon herself to storm Heaven with as many prayers and sacrifices as she could possibly muster for her beloved Audrey. Indeed, her spiritual efforts on behalf of her precious granddaughter were profoundly heroic. Concerning Grandma Nader's nightly vigils, Fr. Emmanuel Charles McCarthy (henceforth referred to as Fr. Emmanuel), a priest of the Byzantine rite of the Melkite Catholic Church and one of the family's spiritual advisors, gives us this account:

> After the accident, Pat Nader would get up at night every hour to say the Rosary for Audrey. Think about it. She would set the clock, get up and pray five decades of the Rosary, and then go back to sleep until the clock went off again the next hour. I don't know how long she did this for Audrey, but it was quite a while.

To make matters worse, some of the treatment Audrey received continued to add to the family's concern and stress. For it was apparent to them that not only did the drugs fail to help Audrey, but they seemed to be counterproductive.

Grandma Nader recalled that Audrey's father told the doctors one day: "You know, you know what you're doing — you're drugging her. You're giving her too many drugs. I don't want you to give her any more drugs." The doctors would get upset, said Grandma Nader, but nevertheless they did what they believed was best for Audrey.

Then, on October 13th, another mishap occurred. The physical therapists administering care to Audrey broke both her legs at the knees, fracturing her tibias. They also dislocated her right shoulder. Ironically, the family discovered the incidents only after ordering the hospital to X-ray Audrey's "swollen knees".

The setbacks distressed the family, but from the darkness some light began to emerge. Linda started to believe in her heart that no matter what anyone else said or thought, the best place for Audrey was at home with her family.

Indeed, Linda believed that Audrey could get better at home. But like before, she continued to meet stiff resistance from the hospital. Finally though, Linda made up her mind and made it official to everyone: Audrey was going home!

"Where are you going to place her?" the hospital wanted to know upon notification that Audrey would defiantly be removed from their care.

"What do you mean, where am I going to place her?" Linda responded in a tone intended to withstand their insinuation that Audrey needed institutionalized care.

"I'm going to place her in my arms," said Linda. "She's going home with me!"

"That's *impossible!*" the doctors replied. "She'll be dead in two weeks!"

"I don't think so," responded Linda. "She's going home!"

The hospital's position was not without merit. According to experts, a move such as Linda proposed actually advanced medical history. By this time, the hospital's position with Audrey had somewhat changed. The doctors admitted that they could do no more and were now open to some form of institutionalized care for Audrey. Likewise, their prognosis now concluded that "*Audrey could live up to two years.*" But, they insisted, home care was out of the question.

In 1987, children with Audrey's condition could not easily receive home care. In fact, at that time home pediatric intensive care unit settings were almost nonexistent, as were pediatric institutional settings. But even if institutionalized care did exist, said Linda's sister Jeri Cox, "Can you imagine a three-year-old in a nursing home?"

Yes, Audrey was going home. Impossible or not, Linda was determined to stick to her decision. Over the four-month period at the University of Massachusetts Medical Center, there was no progress in Audrey's condition. Therefore, by November of 1987, regardless of the experts' evaluations and regardless of the enormity of the responsibility, Audrey Santo was going home, once and for all.

The family sold their two-story home at 1 Rockwood Avenue and moved to 64 South Flagg Street, a predominantly Jewish neighborhood with single-story, ranch-style homes which were better suited to Audrey's needs.

By now, the time for crying was over. The family continued to suffer and pray, but they focused their energy on preparing the new home. There was work to be done. Some remodeling to widen doors and electrical updating were necessary in order to accommodate the critical medical equipment which Audrey would need in her reconstructed room. This equipment included a special bed for postural changes and safety, oxygen and suction machines, a pulse monitor (pulse oximeter), a CO_2 retainer, a specially equipped chair and a ventilator. Although Audrey could breathe on her own, she was partially dependent on a tracheotomy tube in her neck that was connected to a breathing machine. Audrey also required a respirator for carbon dioxide removal.

Likewise, numerous other details needed to be arranged in order to make sure that Audrey received the proper care at home. A staff of professional aides, doctors and nurses would have to be engaged, along with other miscellaneous support and service personnel.

But finally, on November 13, 1987, little Audrey Santo came home from the hospital. To a degree, the nightmare was over.

That afternoon, a small group of relatives and close family friends gathered to welcome Audrey home. Although the hardship and suffering had been great for the family, it was a miracle to have her back again.

"It was just so overwhelming to have her home again," Linda

remembered about that special day. "A lot of people had given up on her, but we never did. We never gave up hope."

While Audrey still suffered from the effects of the broken legs and an ear infection, she immediately seemed to improve at home. Additionally, Linda wanted to change the management of Audrey's medical care and the source of medical advice.

Researching everything she could get her hands on, Linda's efforts led her to the New England Medical Center in Boston. There, advanced video telemetry techniques were utilized in seeking answers to questions about Audrey's particular "brain" states, while further diagnostic tests helped in understanding exactly what her brain had experienced from the accident.

In January of 1988, an extended visit to the New England Medical Center produced a new turn of events. An Arizona specialist, Dr. Edward Kaye, met with Audrey.

Immediately, he found her so captivating and special that he began to call her "Sleeping Beauty". And although Dr. Kaye's examination led to no new medical breakthroughs for Audrey, it did lead to a breakthrough of a different nature.

"What are all these medals," Dr. Kaye inquired, as he couldn't help but notice the dozen or so religious medals attached to two safety pins on Audrey's chest.

"Well," replied Linda, "most of them are from a place in Yugoslavia called Medjugorje. I don't know if you know this, but Our Lady is reportedly appearing there."

Linda proceeded to explain to Dr. Kaye about the apparitions of the Blessed Virgin Mary at Medjugorje. In fact, she, herself and her family had only recently discovered this information.

In October of 1987, about the time that the therapists had broken Audrey's legs, Linda's sister, Jeri, accidentally came across a little tabloid published by Wayne Weible, a Southern Lutheran. The newspaper detailed and chronicled the early events surrounding the Medjugorje apparitions which had begun on June 24, 1981. This was, ironically, the same day that Linda and Stephen Santo had been married.

Jeri became so captivated by the paper that she went to great lengths to copy the entire issue so that she could share it with the family. Thus, one thing led to another, and soon Audrey wore a half-dozen or so Medjugorje medals.

"Are you going to take her there?" Dr. Kaye suddenly inquired as if he intuitively sensed the family's plans for Audrey.

"Well," replied Linda, somewhat puzzled and surprised, "I didn't even think about it."

"Well, you know," offered Dr. Kaye, "I'll write anything you need to do to go there."

Obviously stunned, Linda thanked the doctor and immediately began to contemplate the enormity and challenge of such an effort. Further consultation with the family pediatrician, Dr. Riordan, and a healing priest from Roxbury, Ma., Fr. Edward McDonough who was familiar with Medjugorje, added to the formulation of her decision.

But it was a dream which Linda received in late April that confirmed to her that she should take Audrey to Medjugorje, for it was not like any other dream. "I want to make this clear." said Linda, "I don't receive heavenly messages or visions or anything else. I'm a mom. But I had this dream about this cross. And the cross was lit. The whole cross was lit up. It was a big illuminated cross."

Indeed, it was a very meaningful dream. And for Linda, the vision of the cross meant only one thing. Her decision was made! The next morning Linda told her mother of her plans.

"I need to take Audrey to Medjugorje," Linda enthusiastically explained to Grandma Nader.

"That's crazy," replied her mother. "You can't take her to Medjugorje... That's *impossible!*"

"We've got to take her," insisted Linda. "We've got to figure out a way to take Audrey to Medjugorje."

On July 29, 1988, a Yugoslavian airliner departed from John F. Kennedy Airport in New York City on a nonstop flight to Dubrovnik, Yugoslavia. Aboard the flight was a mother with her ill daughter, once again determined to do the *impossible.*

PART II

LIVING FAITH

CHAPTER SEVEN

HIGHWAY TO HEAVEN

The trip to Medjugorje proved to be a logistical nightmare. To begin with, the Santo family needed $8,000 to pay for traveling expenses for Audrey, Linda and a nurse. On top of that, the details of the trip had to be meticulously arranged in order to ensure Audrey's safety.

But no second-guessing or hesitations occurred on Linda's part. Once she knew in her heart that the trip was God's will, all the other wheels were set in motion without brakes.

It was settled. The three would leave on July 29, 1988 and return on August 12th. This meant that Audrey would be in Medjugorje on the first anniversary of her accident, perhaps, her mother hoped and prayed, to be healed.

Linda decided that traveling on Yugoslavian Airlines (JAT) would be best. JAT gave them a special price and already offered nonstop flights from New York to Dubrovnik. In addition, instead of a jumbo jet, the trip would be aboard a smaller airliner better suited to accommodate their needs.

And their needs were plenty. Linda was forced to purchase a total of six seats because Audrey's condition required that she remain supine throughout the flight. Besides the extra room for Audrey, essential medical equipment necessitated the use of additional seats. A cardiac apnea monitor, suction equipment, stethoscopes, oxygen and numerous boxes of medical supplies accompanied the travelers.

To assist them on their special pilgrimage, Linda and Audrey were joined by Mrs. Joyce O'Neal, R.N., the wife of state Superior Court Judge, Gerald O'Neal of Cape Cod. Mrs. O'Neal was an experienced nurse and was also a good friend.

Finally, after months of planning, the eventful day arrived. Situated in the back of the plane, the three headed across the Atlantic on their mission. Besides the hope they carried in their hearts for Audrey, they also took with them hundreds of petitions from Worcester area residents, including appeals from families of other comatose patients. It was to be a mission of mercy and joy, one that hopefully would bring answers to many prayers, not just their own.

In addition, shortly before their departure, a friend of Linda's, Sister Isabel Bettwy of Steubenville, Ohio, delivered some news which boosted everyone's hopes that something special was in the making for Audrey.

Sister Isabel had traveled to Medjugorje dozens of times, and she had become very close to the visionaries. Her relationship with them permitted her on one occasion to ask Marija Pavlovic Lunetti, one of the Medjugorje visionaries, to offer a picture of Audrey to the Blessed Mother. Reportedly, the Virgin Mary said nothing when she received the picture, but Mary did embrace it in a special way. Linda felt that this was another sign of hope.

"Mary has told many who request a healing to perform a penance or to change their life in some way. Often then, many healings have occurred," said Linda. "Maybe by her embracing Audrey's picture, that was the best answer possible. That showed us that Mary knew about Audrey and loved her."

To say that Mary and all of Heaven knew about Audrey was perhaps an understatement. For the trip to Yugoslavia was not the first effort by the family to obtain a healing through faith for their little girl. Audrey's pictures had been sent to Rome, Ireland, Canada, Lourdes and various locations and shrines known throughout the world for healing.

Likewise, Fr. McDonough of Roxbury, Ma., who Linda attributed her own "healing" many years before, had visited Audrey while she was in the hospital. In fact, Grandma Nader recalled that Fr. McDonough seemed to have worked a miracle then, and they again hoped for one on Audrey's behalf with his help.

"Years ago when Linda was seriously ill," explained Grandma Nader, "the doctors called me and said she probably had just six months to live. We took her to see Fr. McDonough, who was known as a healing priest. Somehow, he picked her out from the crowd. That night, Linda felt strange. Then, the disease was gone and never came back!"

Of course, with such success through faith in the past, it is easy to see how the trip to Medjugorje increasingly became a pilgrimage of hope and trust in God. Indeed, there is no rule that says God can't grant two miracles to the same family.

Not surprisingly, by the time Linda and Audrey departed for Medjugorje, even Grandma Nader's faith in the outcome of the trip was now bordering on euphoria. "I'm excited," she told a Worcester Catholic newspaper that ran a story on the family's departure for Yugoslavia. "I believe very strongly that the baby will wake up."

Thus, Linda and Audrey departed with great confidence, but like all journeys to remote destinations, the trip would have its challenges.

Indeed, the journey to Medjugorje holds challenges for everyone who is "called" there. For just landing at Dubrovnik Airport in the former Yugoslavia is a heart-pounding feat in itself, a test of nerves for all who take this route to the remote Marian shrine.

For years, the beautiful Adriatic coastal seaport of Dubrovnik, with its inner medieval walled city, was a tourist mecca for Eastern Europeans. But with the onset of the apparitions in Medjugorje, thousands of Westerners began flocking to Dubrovnik. Of course, this was never anticipated by the city's planners. Their lack of preparation for such an influx of people is especially evident at the seaside airport in the short runways which extended into the harbor.

To be specific, landing a jumbo jet at Dubrovnik airport often seems to be a miracle itself. The proximity of the nearby mountain range and the strong crosswinds present a challenge for even the best of pilots. And for Western pilgrims who are generally unaccustomed to such a heart-pounding approach and landing, this "initiation" causes one to wonder if God does not deliberately begin the pilgrimage with a check on one's faith.

Additionally, a 1988 arrival in Yugoslavia also presented the anxiety of dealing with the Communist authorities at the airport. For most people, this again was a shock, since smiling faces and hearty welcomes were not to be found. Instead, uniformed soldiers wearing the Red Star of Communism were an instant reminder that this excursion could not to be compared to a Western-style vacation. But for the most part, these minor annoyances passed quickly, and it was on to Medjugorje by bus.

In their case, once out of the airport, Linda, Audrey, and Joyce expected to find an awaiting ambulance. Which they did. However, they quickly discovered to their own dismay that ambulances in Yugoslavia are designed without rear doors. This immediately presented a problem in caring for Audrey. So, Linda and Joyce quickly scrambled to replace the vehicle with an older but more functional government van.

Finally, Audrey was situated and everything was packed, and the little group was off to Medjugorje! But soon another snag developed. The dark green government van contained no air conditioning. Since it was the middle of summer, this situation was almost unbearable. On top of that, the driver insisted that the government forbade him to roll down the windows. Not surprisingly, as the sweltering temperatures rose inside the van, it wasn't too long before Linda was forced to demand that the windows be opened. This courtesy was granted, but only after an extended engagement of differing opinions.

Still, the three-hour ride from Dubrovnik to Medjugorje had its joys, as the scenic beauty of the trip was unforgettable. Many call this trip the "highway to Heaven". For although there are several different routes to Medjugorje, the journey along the Adriatic coastline extending from Dubrovnik northward remains the most popular and scenic way.

For Westerners especially, the trip from Dubrovnik to Medjugorje presents a mixture of breathtaking sights and curious observations. One travels past a collage of limestone alps alternating with intervals of hills, trees and shrub-laden wilderness. With a slight knowledge of history and geography, it is obvious that this terrain is classically Mediterranean, rich in red soil, oak and maple trees, and an assortment of berry vines. For the most part, the area has been the same for centuries. Likewise, the many little rustic towns and villages are delightful, as one immediately notes that everything looks different from America.

But despite the captivating beauty of the physical terrain leading to Medjugorje, it is the faces of the people along the way that undoubtedly leave the deepest impression. Like the work of a sculptor who carefully accentuates key features, the tanned and deeply-lined countenance of the Croatian people is the land's most striking and memorable characteristic, one that almost instantly defines its culture.

Moreover, the faces of the Croatian people reveal the history of the land. While Roman and Greek culture once dominated this region, the people are currently somewhat trapped in a time warp. Their lives reflect centuries of ox-driven carts and little stone homes, while their four official languages (Croatian, Serbian, Macedonian and Slovenian) and two alphabets (Latin and Cyrillic) are further evidence of the former Yugoslavia's stagnant condition.

Living century-old lifestyles which provide income and food, most of the people of these rustic towns and villages tend to their cows, sheep, chickens and goats during the day. Most have little stucco homes with a stable attached and some land for the animals to graze. Some cultivate fields of tobacco and grapes, others have prosperous little gardens, while still others simply tend to their homes. On a summer day, people can be seen resting, as "siesta" is still a tradition.

But progress has not left these people completely untouched. There are some larger and more developed cities, such as Dubrovnik and Zagreb. Likewise, some rural homes are built to more modern standards, with Western-style kitchens and bathrooms. Most people own cars, color TV's, VCR's, telephones, washers and dryers. Local discotheques are scattered everywhere, and the young people outwardly reflect Western culture with their taste in cigarettes, clothing, hairstyles and entertainment.

During much of the twentieth century, the Croatian, Serbian and Muslim people in former Yugoslavia had found themselves politically enslaved by Marshall Tito's brand of Communism.

While his particular flavor of oppression was a little less restrictive than that of neighboring Albania, former Yugoslavians have nonetheless lived with fifty years of forced rule and pretentious class struggle. The western part of Bosnia, where Medjugorje sits, is primarily inhabited by Roman Catholic Croats. And often, over the centuries, it has taken violence to ensure their viability.

A bit of historical insight helps to better understand the rough yet sensitive essence of these people. During World War II, Yugoslavia was split apart by totalitarian extremists and invading forces. The Nazis occupied the country and nurtured right-wing elements, while Tito led a Marxist force that promoted and enforced the ideals of an atheistic left wing. Out of a population of almost 15 million, 1.7 million were killed. Century-old internal rifts were exacerbated during the war, thus leading to the modern-day tensions.

While Yugoslavia was perhaps the most open Eastern-block country before the fall of the Iron Curtain, according to Amnesty International, it had the most political prisoners. In 1991, this tension once again bubbled to the surface, causing the most brutal, bloody and ruthless war on European soil since World War II.

Overall, the faces of the people are careworn and war-torn, and it is evident that the harsh, unpredictable state of their lives has taken its toll.

And not surprisingly, they hunger in a profound way to be permanently liberated from this chronic misery.

CHAPTER EIGHT

THE GOSPA

For many pilgrims, the three-hour journey from Dubrovnik to Medjugorje can be quite strenuous. The old highway is rather in disrepair, and the buses that carry the pilgrims are somewhat inferior by Western standards; nonetheless, the winding road eventually slides between the mountains, and soon enough Medjugorje is in sight.

"Medjugorje" is a Slavic word that literally means "between the mountains". The neighboring village, Bijakovici, sits at the base of the two hills of Crnica and Podbrdo. Like Medjugorje, Bijakovici is a small village of white stone houses, tobacco fields and grape vineyards. And like Bosnia itself, the joined villages of Medjugorje and Bijakovici have a curious past of conflicts and vendettas that are rooted in history and blood.

Yet, in spite of the internal struggles, the Catholic residents of these villages all share St. James Church as their place of worship. St. James Church actually serves the needs of about 530 families from five villages.

This unusually large church in the village of Medjugorje was built from 1937 to 1969. During its construction, many people wondered why it was being built so big. Although none could say for sure, one villager supposedly saw the church prefigured in a vision, and he claimed to have seen the Madonna floating above it.

Several hundred families comprise the village of Medjugorje, and with the four surrounding villages, all blend into one medium-size town. For hundreds of years, the Church and the faith have been the center of the people's lives, along with one of their holiest devotion sites, Mt. Krizevac.

This mountain with its heavy foliage sits at the rear of the villages and towers 1,300 meters high. In 1933, the villagers erected a huge, cement cross on its summit in honor of the nineteen hundredth anniversary of Christ's death; since that time, it has become known as "Cross Mountain".

Long before the apparitions at Medjugorje, Mt. Krizevac was a focal point for prayer. This is especially evident in the fixed tablets which display the Stations of the Cross along the steep, rocky path up the mountain. It's a strenuous climb that takes at least a half-hour to complete, and may take more than two hours for the elderly or handicapped. But once atop the summit of Mt. Krizevac, the view is breathtaking.

Indeed, though the land around Medjugorje is poor and undeveloped, the Creator's handiwork is easily recognizable. Waves of colored fields and rolling hills poetically intertwine for miles in every direction, as sweet winds carry pleasant aromas of vineyards and gardens. In the distance, mountain ranges with snow-capped peaks are reminiscent of giant natural sentinels, perhaps fashioned by God to protect and surround the priceless and holy terrain. The pilgrims say, the entire area is a spectacle of fascinating contrast and beauty.

In Medjugorje, everyday life had seen little change for centuries; yet, the dawn of June 24, 1981 was incredibly different.

The events of that particular morning would bring rapid and lasting changes to the area as never before experienced.

A horrendously violent thunderstorm with lightning, rain and hail blew in with a force and intensity so strong that it frightened even the hearty villagers. Some people said that it reminded them of Judgment Day, while others paralleled the strange events to prophecies foretold in the Book of Revelation. One woman emotionally fought back her fear by splashing holy water in all directions just in case the storm was of a diabolical origin.

June 24th was a Wednesday, the feast of Saint John the Baptist. About 4:00 p.m., two local teenage girls, Ivanka Ivankovic and Mirjana Dragicevic, were on their way home from a sheep pasture.

It was a trip they had made many times before along the rocky path of the hill known as Podbrdo.

Suddenly, Ivanka saw a glowing silhouette. It was a distinct shape. In the center, a young lady in a gray robe, whose face glowed, seemed to materialize.

"Mirjana, look!" cried Ivanka. "It's the Gospa (Our Lady)!"

"Don't be idiotic," replied Mirjana.

At first Mirjana didn't bother to look. But seconds later, she did. And there, before her eyes, she saw the apparition. Together, the girls quickly fled from the sight.

Later, when they mustered up the courage to return with others, they discovered that "the apparition" was truly the "Gospa", the Blessed Virgin Mary.

The word spread quickly. Soon, pilgrims from all over the world came to see. To put it mildly, the Communists didn't like it, so the government persecuted both the children and the Franciscan priests at St. James Church, even going so far as to detain them. Although the local bishop was at first sympathetic, he quickly changed into the greatest foe of the apparitions. His current successor maintains his skeptical attitude.

Over the years, the supernatural has consistently meshed with the natural world in Medjugorje, and more than twenty million people from all religions, races and nations have come to see for themselves this bit of Heaven on earth. Many visitors have claimed to witness the incredible. They say that angels, words and figures made of clouds sometimes appeared overhead, while the sun danced and changed colors just as it did at Fatima.

Curiously similar to Linda Santo's dream, many people have claimed to see the huge, thirty-foot cross on Mt. Krizevac elevate and spin at night, while simultaneously glowing with supernatural, fluorescent light. On the hills mysterious fires, which would vanish upon close inspection, were also witnessed.

Although skeptics have surfaced, they have been relatively few in number. Many prominent theologians and Mariologists have given favorable opinions regarding the events, methodically disarming and muting critics. Likewise, the local bishop's attempt to deflate the importance of the visions was erased by Rome's call for a new commission to investigate them. This commission eventually ruled for continued observation of the events which have had such a lasting impression on so many.

However, one aspect of Medjugorje has left the deepest mark. Throughout the world millions have returned home permanently changed, their lives either newly or more profoundly converted to God. The Virgin's call to prayer, penance, faith, fasting and peace has been deeply internalized and answered by many. New entities called "Peace Centers" have cropped up around the globe. These Peace Centers are devoted exclusively to spreading the message of Medjugorje and other Marian apparitions. All this has happened in response to the Virgin's requests at Medjugorje to "**live and spread**" her messages.

Moreover, this was exactly how and why Linda's sister, Jeri Cox, learned about Medjugorje in the first place. For Wayne Weible, a then Protestant journalist, had printed and distributed over twenty million copies of his little newspaper in response to Mary's call. The impact of this well-written, objective documentary on the Medjugorje events became unsurpassed, as repeatedly, groups of pilgrims were led to search for an encounter with their spiritual mother who was now appearing in Medjugorje. But the fact that so many have actually traveled to Medjugorje can only be credited to God. For it was God's idea to send the Blessed Virgin Mary to this little Croatian village in "the middle of nowhere", and then to call His children there.

Not surprisingly, that's exactly where Linda felt she was when they finally arrived in Medjugorje that mid-afternoon of July 30, 1988. For from what she could observe, she was indeed in "the middle of nowhere" like never before!

But everything soon came together. Linda and Joyce quickly discovered that they were the only pilgrims staying with a "very nice" family of five, although the sole family member who spoke English was a fourteen year-old girl named Zorica. They had a perfect view from a new room with its own bathroom. They soon also learned that their house was within a short walking distance of St. James Church, and in the opposite direction stood Mt. Krizevac and Apparition Hill.

Likewise, the sight of Audrey's face in the moon on both Friday and Saturday nights was very special; moreover, the phenomenon especially added to Linda's anticipation. For she believed that it was perhaps another sign, a sign that Audrey would be healed. Indeed, Linda began to increasingly believe that Audrey would be healed on the one-year anniversary of her accident.

And so, while Medjugorje's church, people, culture, history and terrain were captivating, shortly after Linda arrived, her first priority again began to consume her complete attention.

She had come for Audrey. She had come for Audrey's healing. And in spite of the fact that the wonders of Medjugorje were truly mystifying, fascinating and alluring, the days of waiting were more than she could take.

But on Sunday night, July 31, 1988, the moment had finally arrived. Just as they had hoped, Linda, Joyce and Audrey arrived at St. James Church in Medjugorje and were led up the steps and into the apparition room of the choir loft, where moments later, the Queen of Peace paid the world — and one sick little girl — a very special visit.

CHAPTER NINE

A DECIDING MOMENT

While the daring trip demanded attention to every detail for the sake of Audrey's physical well-being, Linda had not been remiss in arranging the most important aspect of their visit to Medjugorje: permission for Audrey to be in St. James Church during the apparitions of the Virgin Mary.

Linda felt that such a privilege was critical. Indeed, any mother who seeks what she believes to be best for her child cannot be faulted. But it must be noted that with strong faith and in accordance with God's will, pilgrims who have traveled to Marian shrines such as Lourdes, Fatima and Medjugorje in search of healing have received those very healings in a variety of places, everywhere from apparition rooms to hotel rooms. The graces and the healings come, often unexpectedly and unpredictably, according to God's perfect plan, not man's.

At Lourdes, where thousands of healings have been reported (which include many approved healings, i.e., those that have been officially documented), the greatest number of miracles seem to occur when the priests bless the sick with the Blessed Sacrament. Most noteworthy is the fact that these blessings are not given at the apparition site, nor at the famous healing baths.

Likewise in Medjugorje, miraculous healings have been reported at various locations — inside St. James Church, on the top of Mt. Krizevac, and along the pathways of Apparition Hill. Just as at

Lourdes, God has not limited Himself to only a few locations to render such graces at Medjugorje.

But in her desire to do the very best for Audrey, Linda undauntingly telephoned the rectory of St. James Church all the way from her home in Worcester several months in advance of their trip. She wanted to prearrange Audrey's permission to be admitted into the church at the time of the daily apparition. Linda believed that she had to do this because she had been cautioned that Audrey would never be able to get into the church due to the huge crowds that attend the evening Mass. However, Heaven was already ahead of her. When Linda called, she received a special invitation.

Elucidating her decision to phone the rectory of St. James Church, Linda said:

> Don't forget, I'm a mother. When people started to tell me there would be thousands of people in Medjugorje and that they were not going to be able to get Audrey even into the church, well, I decided, this is crazy, I'm going to call the rectory at Medjugorje.
>
> So, I called and some woman answered the phone and didn't understand what I was saying. But, another woman who could speak English was put on the phone. I then told her, "I just want to get Audrey, my child, into the church. She will be on a stretcher and we have some medical equipment. If we could just have some space in the church..."
>
> I wasn't looking to get into the apparition room or seeking any special favor. We just wanted to get into the church. But then, the woman came back to the phone after checking with someone, and she said, "Father Pervan said that you are invited into the apparition room."

It was exhilarating news. But Linda had to politely explain that, as yet, no date had been set for the trip. Still, it didn't matter. The woman assured her that when they arrived at the church, Audrey would be invited into the apparition room. And that was exactly what happened.

Thus, early Sunday evening, July 31, 1988, equipped with all the necessities and especially their prayers and hopes, Linda, Joyce and Audrey began to make their way to St. James Church for the 6:40 p.m. apparition.

By this time, Linda's spirits were soaring. Audrey had received incredible attention from literally dozens of English, Irish, Italian, German and Croatian pilgrims. On a nonstop basis they had visited her during her first two days in Medjugorje. This special attention, along with the miraculous image of Audrey's face in the moon, convinced Linda that God was planning a miracle.

"I figured Our Lady was going to go to Jesus and have Audrey healed," said Linda, recalling her thoughts on that particular evening. "That's what I thought. What would you think? With the sight of her face in the moon, I thought, 'Well, we're going to have a miracle.' I even brought her little sandals with me so that she could put them on to run up the mountain afterward."

All the medical equipment required that Linda and Joyce arrange for a taxicab to drive them to the church that evening. An American priest from Worcester, Fr. John, and Zorica, the English-speaking Croatian girl, agreed to meet them there. They would help carry everything upstairs to the apparition room.

Upon arrival at St. James Church, Audrey was carried through a side door near the front of the church and then up a steep stairwell to the choir loft. She was then placed directly below the exact location where Our Lady was to appear. With this, as thousands of the faithful prayed and sang in the main portion of the church below, the long-awaited moment had arrived.

Slowly, after everyone was situated, Linda, Zorica, Joyce and the priest began to pray and to wait for the visionaries who were coming to the church that evening. Several minutes later, Fr. Slavko Barbaric and one of the visionaries, Ivan Dragicevic, entered, knelt down and began to pray. Fr. Barbaric and Ivan were "very nice" and cordial to the visitors. Other than that, Linda remembered nothing remarkable except that the heat in the choir loft grew unbearable, as it had in the van during their journey from Dubrovnik to Medjugorje. However, an unexplainable mystery concerning the excruciating heat surrounded little Audrey.

For some reason, while everyone else was baking from the rising temperature, not a drop of perspiration exuded from Audrey's body. In addition, the child's hair appeared to be slightly flowing, as if a breeze traveled through it. Yet, when they had traveled from the Dubrovnik airport to Medjugorje, Linda noted that "Audrey was sweating like everybody else."

For the record, the St. James Church choir loft is actually a very simple and almost empty room with an old organ resting in one corner. Linda also recalled noticing a crucifix hanging in the center of the wall directly below where Mary was to appear.

Then, a few minutes after Ivan and Fr. Barbaric had arrived, it became apparent that Ivan was in ecstasy. The apparition had begun. Although no one else could see the Virgin Mary, everyone in the room believed that she was present, invisibly towering in front and above all of them.

Although Ivan Dragicevic said nothing specific to Audrey before the apparition, he did acknowledge her just before he went into ecstasy. But during the apparition, however, each person was left to enjoy their own unique encounter with Heaven's Queen.

"Everybody was having their own personal experiences," recalled Linda. "It was very emotional. When Ivan went into ecstasy and Our Lady appeared, I cried, we all cried. The apparition lasted about seven to ten minutes."

While Linda sensed that Audrey was somehow communicating with the Virgin, her own petitions to Mary were painful yet profound revelations of her heartfelt sorrow and love for Audrey, for Linda asked the Mother of God *"to either heal my daughter or take her."*

Although nothing else particularly memorable happened during the apparition, something curious did occur after it had ended. Immediately after coming out of ecstasy, Ivan stood up and then suddenly moved over and knelt down next to Audrey. He then spoke to her for about five minutes in Croatian. It was a stunning yet mysterious conversation. Neither Linda nor anyone else knew what Ivan was saying to Audrey. "I never found out and I never asked him," said Linda. "I figured if I were supposed to know, he'd tell me. He spoke to her quite a while."

After Ivan finished speaking to Audrey, the invited guests then carried the little girl back down the steps to the front of St. James Church. There, they were immediately inundated by the crowd, many of whom often seek to touch anyone who has attended the evening apparition in the loft. According to Linda, they literally had to fight to leave, because some people attempted to grab Audrey.

Finally, after getting back to their accommodations, everyone began to relax and absorb what had occurred. It had been an incredibly powerful and emotional experience. But at the same time, they realized that Audrey had not been healed. Still, no one was ready to give up hope, for the week was not yet over.

During the next couple days, Linda used her available time to canvass the village and hills that make up Medjugorje. People would stop to talk to her all the time, and on Monday evening she even attended a special apparition on Podbrdo. But Audrey never left her mind, as she spent all night that Monday praying the Rosary for her.

Then, three days after the apparition, on Wednesday, August 4, 1988, Linda, Joyce and Audrey returned to St. James Church for a second apparition. Once again, it was to be a critical evening in the life of little Audrey Santo.

That night, a radio broadcaster named Don Devaney from Dublin, Ireland, carried Audrey up the steps into the apparition room. His role was one of those curious and unexplainable coincidences that often happen at Medjugorje; Mr. Devaney was the father of a four year-old daughter also named Audrey.

Once in the apparition room, everyone took their places. Audrey was again placed in front of Ivan and directly below the anticipated site of the apparition of the Virgin Mary. Joyce O'Neal recalled that, once more, it was a very special moment. "This big Irish fellow carried Audrey up to the loft. But Audrey was uncommonly quiet and still that night," said Joyce," There was an aura of holiness there. You could feel the spirituality. It was very moving."[1]

Unlike Sunday, it was a long apparition, twenty minutes or more. Afterwards, Ivan again immediately spoke to Audrey for approximately five minutes. And again, no one knew what was said. Recalled Joyce, "Ivan came over and knelt beside Audrey. But we couldn't understand him. And then I was slain in the spirit right after the apparition. There was this fullness, this feeling of peace there."[2]

After this they all headed back to their lodgings. And as with the first apparition, nothing had occurred with Audrey - nothing until Audrey, Linda and Joyce returned to their room.

Suddenly, within a couple of hours of the apparition, Audrey started to become animated. Something was happening to her. Her head and hands began to move. Her pupils equalized and she started reacting to light. Then, Audrey's eyes started tracking her nurse, Joyce. To the best of their opinion, everyone there thought that Audrey was perhaps coming out of her coma-like state.

For Linda, it was an indescribable moment of intense emotion. "We were screaming. We were hysterical. We were praising the Lord," said Linda. "We were thanking the Blessed Mother. We figured Audrey was going to get up! We figured she was about to be healed!"

Within minutes, their Croatian hosts came rushing upstairs, and everyone began hugging and kissing one another. Indeed, it was a euphoric moment of celebration and joy.

But then, it all ended. Suddenly, Audrey fell back onto the bed and her eyes closed. Her body totally ceased moving, as if she had fallen into a deep sleep.

"She became lifeless," said Linda, "everything stopped."

"We couldn't see her breathing," recalled Joyce. "Her lungs weren't expanding. She wasn't getting any air." [3]

Quickly, Joyce and Linda scrambled to find a stethoscope. Each took a turn listening to Audrey's heart. Soon, their worst fears were confirmed.

Audrey had "coded" — her heartbeat and pulse could not be found. She had stopped breathing. And in seconds, the roomful of people went from sheer ecstasy to pure agony.

CHAPTER TEN

"GOD DOES PROVIDE"

The situation was desperate. In the United States, established emergency help exists in almost every community, but Audrey, Linda and Joyce were in a rural, mountainous village in the middle of Yugoslavia with no 9-1-1 service at their fingertips.

Fortunately, the two women were experienced in this kind of crisis, and by the grace of God, they didn't panic. Together, Linda and Joyce managed to get Audrey breathing again. Then, after resuscitating her and detecting her pulse, they administered oxygen. Soon, others came to help, including an Italian doctor. Linda recalled the urgency of the moment: "When you go into cardiac arrest, everything stops, your heart, your lungs...everything. We did some compressions, and in a couple of minutes her heartbeat came back, she was back to life. Thank God."

But although Audrey was breathing on her own, Linda and Joyce knew that they needed to get her to a hospital quickly. They also understood that their pilgrimage to Medjugorje was over.

As fast as possible, Linda contacted Zorica's father and the four of them rode in his car to the nearest hospital in a town named Citluk. It was a half-hour drive and Audrey cried along the way. But when they arrived, they discovered that the hospital carried no oxygen.

They then drove several hours from Citluk to a hospital in Zagreb. But this time, they were denied admission. Finally, Linda and Joyce decided to drive back to Mostar, a city only twenty miles from Medjugorje.

Meanwhile, Audrey began to choke and "coded" five more times during the hectic attempts to find a hospital suitable for her. Indeed, it was one life and death situation after another, leaving Linda and Joyce physically and emotionally exhausted.

"It was incredible," said Linda. "We were going back and forth, back and forth, to these hospitals. And Audrey kept going in and out. It felt like an eternity before Audrey stabilized."

"I thought we were going to be killed," remembered Joyce. "This car had very poor brakes. And we were speeding down these mountainous roads from Medjugorje to Mostar. We were exhausted. I had about five hours of sleep in a week. I really didn't think Audrey would get back alive."[1]

While the Mostar hospital finally proved to be a solution, it wasn't one that Linda and Joyce were comfortable with. The Communist-controlled facility was antiquated, something out of the 1950's by Western standards. And, what Audrey needed most — oxygen — was in limited supply.

There was another disturbing aspect about the Mostar facility: It was the primary abortion clinic in Yugoslavia, catering to the free slaughter of unborn infants from all of Eastern Europe. Although the staff was wonderful, the facility itself inspired more fear than calm.

Said Linda:

The hospital was a nightmare, just to look at. We got there on Wednesday night, and by Thursday afternoon the doctors were getting aggravated because we were using up all the oxygen in the hospital. They didn't like that.

But you had to have seen this place. There was no lab or X-ray. There was blood on the walls. There was blood on the sheets. There were wires hanging out of the walls. Everything was dirty. There were bugs, no fans and no air conditioners. They had a typewriter from the 1920's.

It was a Communist government-run facility. They didn't feed you. Patients were not bathed and everything they did there was the minimal. They had one hot plate for Turkish coffee, no paper cups, no towels or washcloths. The patients' beds were never changed until they left. There were no trash cans. Everyone smoked. There was one phone that was about twenty years old. There were no disposables and no scissors. They used razor blades to cut everything. There was one stethoscope and one phone on every floor. Every piece of equipment was over thirty years old. Basically, what happens is you don't go there to get well, you go there to die. The place looked like Auschwitz. And you know, they thought we were nuts.

Joyce concurred. To her, the entire series of events was uncanny. "The whole scene was unbelievable," said Joyce. "We ended up in a hospital in Mostar. The hospital had no penicillin, no hot water and no air conditioning. We had the only air-conditioned room. It was pre-World War II. It was the wildest scene. The first night there, at the hospital, the doctors came smoking cigarettes, and then they were leaning on the oxygen tank as they smoked. But, the one doctor was excellent."[2]

Not surprisingly, Linda also began to think that she was nuts for even being there. So once Audrey had stabilized, she immediately attempted to return to the United States.

But another snag quickly developed. Yugoslavian Airlines (JAT) wouldn't take them, nor would any other commercial airline. This was due to concerns over any liability the airline might incur because of Audrey's perilous condition.

So Linda called her sister, Jeri, whose oldest daughter, Cindy, searched for a political solution in Massachusetts. But again, it wasn't easy.

U.S. Senator Ted Kennedy of Massachusetts didn't want to hear anything about it, and his office made it clear that they had no desire to help or get involved. Likewise, several other avenues of potential political help proved fruitless.

Finally, Massachusetts Congressman Joseph Early took charge and managed to resolve their plight using the Presidential MED EVAC airplane. This Air Force special-detail plane, together with a medical team, was stationed in Frankfurt, Germany. Through

Representative Early's intercession, it was commissioned to fly to Mostar to pick up Audrey, Linda and Joyce and then to fly them back to Frankfurt. The very next day this was exactly what happened.

Then, on Friday, August 6th, after a brief hospital stay in Germany, the government plane flew them to Andrews Air Force Base outside of Washington, D.C.

All in all, it was an exhausting experience, but Audrey made it back to America alive. Recalled Linda:

Congressman Early's secretary, Louise Buchanan, worked very hard, and they got us home. It took a lot of work. They had to get the plane, clear Communist airways, pick us up in Mostar and get us back to the United States. It took a lot of work by a lot of people.

There was an intensive care unit, ten male nurses, a pediatrician, a cardiologist and a respiratory therapist on the Presidential MED EVAC flight. They stabilized Audrey, and after we got to the hospital in Germany, they thought she was pretty good, so we flew from Germany back to the United States.

The family secured a mortgage for $25,000 and was able to arrange for a small medically equipped plane to bring Audrey back home. Accompanied by a respiratory therapist, she was flown from Andrews Air Force Base to Worcester. Her pediatrician, Dr. Riordan, then arranged for Audrey to be transferred to St. Vincent's Hospital by ambulance.

Once again, the police prearranged for the streets to be road blocked, and a motorcade escorted Audrey to St. Vincent's Hospital. Fortunately, the urgency on this trip wasn't as acute, and consequently, the entire affair even evoked a lighter side by an accident of fate.

Democratic Presidential candidate and former Massachusetts Governor, Michael Dukakis, just happened to be campaigning that day in Worcester. Noticing the street blockades for Audrey's ambulance, one of the medics quipped, "The press is gonna think Dukakis has a broken fingernail and we're rushing him to the hospital."

Of course, the media was not deceived by the motorcade. They picked up on the whole affair because of all the fuss, and they were waiting at the hospital. The following day, Audrey made the news once more.

On the plus side, though, Audrey stayed just one night at St. Vincent's Hospital and was then dismissed. The next day, the exhausted family returned to their home at 64 South Flagg Street in Worcester. They were disappointed, yet relieved at the same time.

But Linda's own spiritual life and faith were greatly strengthened through the trip to Medjugorje. God used this experience to continue to teach her about His ways. A brief excerpt from her journal shows a glimpse of just how much God was working in her at this time. Wrote Linda:

> Most people go to Medjugorje to see the signs to show them there is a God and to confirm the authenticity of the apparitions. I went to Medjugorje for peace, spiritual renewal and the healing of Audrey. I believed quite firmly that all three would happen. I was graced by many signs, not the same ones that I have heard people talk about. But hopefully, I received the true meaning of this most holy place. The real message of Medjugorje is to do penance, pray and to fast, all of which I did and saw. We must desire to love God fully, and in doing this, we must have incredible faith. God does provide and He does love us, but we must return this love to God, even in the small human ways. The people of Medjugorje are living examples of penance and prayer without reservation. We, too, must be this way.

All things considered, the trip to Medjugorje had been a success for both Audrey and Linda, though it was simultaneously a very difficult experience. And although Audrey did not receive a healing, she returned alive, thus maintaining Linda's hope and faith that God was still planning to answer her prayers.

PART III

BAPTIZED IN CHRIST

CHAPTER ELEVEN

POSITIVE SIGNS

Home sweet home. By Saturday, August 7th, Linda and Audrey were back home in Worcester, Massachusetts, ready to put behind them the stress and fatigue of the previous seventy-two hours.

While Audrey had not been miraculously healed in Medjugorje, in many ways it was a wonder that she had successfully endured the grueling trip. Audrey's nurse, Joyce O'Neal, wished to emphasize just this. "It was a miracle she got back alive," said Joyce. "In the hospital in Mostar, they said she wasn't going to make it."

According to Joyce, the doctors in Mostar were convinced that Audrey would die, just like some other doctors had prognosticated once before. But they did not reveal their opinions to Linda. Joyce said, "The doctors never thought Audrey would get out of there alive. But they didn't want Linda to know. 'Baby die, baby die,' they would say to me when Linda wasn't near, 'Baby die.'"[1]

Indeed, considering the fact that Audrey had survived a half dozen cardiac arrests, there was nothing left to do except to praise and thank the Lord. Audrey appeared no worse-off from the whole ordeal. Most of all, the family was still prepared to continue to give her all the love, care and prayers she needed to get better. But, this was not an easy endeavor to undertake.

In their hearts, the Santo family never wavered in their desire to care for Audrey at home. But in reality, the day-to-day, week-to-week, full-time attention that Audrey needed proved to be quite demanding.

The greatest adjustment was regularly having so many extra people in the house, as a team of nurses was needed to care for Audrey around the clock. While the nurses were responsible for many things, their most routine duty was the constant suctioning of saliva from Audrey's mouth approximately every three or four minutes. In addition, they were required to clean, feed (through a twelve-inch gastric tube directly entering the stomach) and turn Audrey as necessary or as scheduled.

Along with the nurses, there also was a constant flow of doctors, respiratory therapists, physical therapists and delivery people to and from the Santo home. This commotion continued throughout the day, every day.

Thus, almost like the accident itself, Audrey's home care proved to be a difficult ordeal for the family. Indeed, adequate attention to Audrey's needs generated a fair amount of stress, especially in the beginning before the family acquired the twenty four-hour nursing staff.

About all the care, activity and traffic in their home, Linda said:

We're human. Sometimes it can be really taxing, especially on the kids when they want some privacy. There is no privacy. When we can grab some, we grab it. This certainly has changed our lives. We're still close. However, the stress level is different.

But after we brought Audrey to the new home, she really improved. She needed acute care. But at home, she really began to improve. Still, we had to be there all the time.

But even before the trip to Medjugorje, Audrey was showing indications of improvement. Though still a prisoner of the coma-like state, her physical actions revealed some slight changes which her doctors acknowledged as positive. In retrospect, these improvements confirmed that the decision to move Audrey home was the correct one.

60

According to several different family members, Audrey became much less tense after she arrived home. In the hospital, she had been very stiff. But once at home, Audrey's hands and body became more relaxed. Her head began to turn, and when she was in pain, her face began to express her sadness.

Another positive sign that appeared after Audrey returned home was her response to sensory stimulation. Audrey's Aunt Jeri said, "Audrey would feel pain and she responded to it by moving from the source. She also seemed to respond to pleasure. She responded to light, and her eyes appeared to focus. She also began to respond to loud noises."

Moreover, the doctors' notes clearly indicate that once at home, Audrey regularly began to respond to voices. She also seemed to sense when someone was present. By gently squeezing a hand or through her eye movement, she began to communicate. On occasion, she would even turn over in bed, and she would exhibit a twitching type of movement when frustrated. Most importantly, Audrey regained the five pounds she had lost during her first few weeks in the hospital. She also returned to her normal sleeping patterns.

Deborah Fournier, R.N., one of Audrey's nurses, noted that Audrey became very emotionally aware of her surroundings. Like any other child, she got mad, happy, or sad. She even cried when hurt or disappointed. These emotions, said Deborah, were very discernible especially when Grandma Nader was there. "I especially noticed that when her Grandmother came into the room," said Deborah, "you could tell right way that she was happy and didn't want her to leave."[2]

Overall, Audrey definitely showed significant improvement and her family was thrilled. "These seem like such little things," said Jeri Cox, "but they mean so much to someone recovering from this type of coma condition."

Most remarkably, Audrey has never shown any signs of bedsores, and her lab tests have been consistent, showing no change from the beginning. The doctors say that this is extraordinary for someone confined to bed.

"There's been no red marks on her," said Linda. "She's growing normally and her blood and urine tests have all been normal. She's healthy. It's just that she's like 'Sleeping Beauty'. She doesn't wake up."

Indeed, "Sleeping Beauty" describes little Audrey Santo perfectly. For Audrey's golden-brown hair, rosy cheeks and her neat, glowing and healthy appearance seem to contrast remarkably with what one would expect to find from a child in such a state. To the experts, these characteristics have been especially extraordinary. But for others, there is an answer.

Said Father Emmanuel:

Love, pure love has been behind the enormous physical and spiritual care for Audrey that is going on. This has been the story here, this magnificent care. My first impressions were: these ordinary Christians are doing great deeds of love and receiving nothing. For there is staggering difficulty in this, to choose sacrifical love in a world built around organized lovelessness. The Santo home is an atmosphere of goodness and incredible Christian love. It is very difficult to take care of people in a coma. It is an ordeal. The lack of response from people in a coma requires enormous love, for there is no love coming back. There is no gratitude. This is an ordeal in the extreme.

From the beginning, the extraordinary "exceptions" to Audrey's condition have intrigued and baffled the experts observing her. From her glowing hair to the absence of bedsores and brain seizures, Audrey's condition has been unique. But it has been more than just the unique physical aspects of her case that have intrigued her family. For right from the start, on the very day of the accident, there also appeared to be a series of secondary events unfolding around Audrey that, like her unique health and beauty, almost deliberately drew attention to her.

While the broad media attention attracted by the accident on the first day is not uncommon for such life and death emergencies, its persisting endurance has been exceptional. Through a series of newspaper articles, feature stories and television reports, the Worcester media have not let Audrey out of their sight.

The extent of coverage outside of Worcester has also been

remarkable. Although there are drownings in pools or at the ocean almost every day on the east coast, the story of Audrey's ordeal was reported in newspapers as far away as Maine. A collection of newspaper clippings, received and compiled by the Santo family, reveals that Audrey's drowning became a news item carried, circulated and updated by the wire services. Tiny newspaper clippings were constantly sent to the family from all over the east coast. Consequently, the media attention also stimulated an incredible outpouring of financial support for Audrey and her family.

The cost of Audrey's care has been astronomical, and the insurance went only so far. Fortunately, the tremendous media focus soon resulted in benefits, bake sales, raffles, concerts, dances, donation drives and a special fund to help offset the enormous debt the family was incurring. Over time, the Massachusetts Institute for the Blind eventually supplemented this effort by declaring Audrey eligible for benefits.

But to the Santo family, there was something even more going on around Audrey, something unexplainable — something, said Linda, that appeared to be coming from God.

Proof of this became particularly evident when people offered to help in many ways, and especially when a diverse number of groups began to publicly proclaim that they were now praying for little Audrey. Not only were they praying, but they were also fasting and beseeching God for Audrey's healing.

The reports were remarkable. A local Mormon group from the Church of the Latter Day Saints began to pray and fast each weekend for Audrey's recovery. A group of Baptists, who would regularly come to the Santo house to pray, did the same. There were Jews from synagogues, worshipers from Pentecostal, Presbyterian, Catholic and Greek Orthodox Churches, and several religious communities, who also announced their intentions to aid Audrey's healing through the power of intercessory prayer.

On top of all this, many individuals who admitted that they "hadn't prayed" for anything or anyone in years said that they were now praying for Audrey. Some Catholics reported that because of Audrey, they had returned to the Sacraments and the Rosary. A twenty-five-year-old Baptist woman from Shrewbury, who was a former coma patient, came to visit Audrey. She claimed that during her own comatose period, she had visited Jesus, and for some reason, she strongly believed that "Audrey, too was visiting with Jesus."

In Linda's eyes, everything began to converge, and she began to feel in her heart that perhaps something special was unfolding around and through the life of her daughter. Linda said:

At the hospital, on the day of the accident, I had an indication that there was something special happening there, something special with Audrey and the Lord. We were in trauma, in shock, yet there were all these TV and radio people there. A week after the accident, there were people already coming to pray and fast. We didn't know these people. It was a communal response, but it was incredible, it was extraordinary. It's without a doubt amazing how so many people of so many faiths have been brought together through our crisis. It should prove that God is here with us and He's the same God for us all. This is something that should strengthen our faith.

Indeed, a strong faith was obviously something that Linda already possessed. Like her parents, she had always approached her life more through the eyes of her soul than her body. And so, it was with this spiritual instinct that Linda began to conclude that the events surrounding Audrey were apparently not the end results of an accident, but the beginning stages ... of a miracle.

CHAPTER TWELVE

NURTURING SOULS

Over the months, the overwhelming response and the profound outpouring of support and prayers signified that something very curious was unfolding. And Linda Santo was not the only one who noticed this. A local newspaper reporter, Neil Isakson, wrote in a published story, *"Why has there been so much attention focused on this four-year-old, as opposed to another who may have suffered just as unfortunate an accident?"*[1]

All in all, by the time Audrey returned home from the hospital in November 1987, Linda had begun to suspect that her daughter's accident was being used by God in a divine way that exceeded human understanding. This belief of hers was reinforced by a curious comment made by a priest who visited Audrey in the hospital immediately after the accident. Fr. Leo Berry, who was close to the family, told Linda, *"You have your saint."*

But although the pieces were beginning to appear, the greater picture surrounding the life and tragic accident of Audrey Santo was still puzzling. However, by November of 1987, Linda was already stepping out in faith and openly advancing her heartfelt belief that Audrey was chosen for a mission, a heavenly mission known only to God.

Six months later, it was obvious that this feeling of Linda's had intensified. For not only were the details of Audrey's trip to

Medjugorje reported in the newspapers, but reporters were now also chronicling Linda's confidence in the events at Medjugorje. Her confidence presented a strong witness to the public regarding the authenticity of the apparitions at Medjugorje and reflected her continued belief that her daughter's life held a special meaning.

Quoting Linda about Medjugorje, one newspaper reported: *"Ms. Santo, who said she has always maintained a faith in 'miracles and miraculous recoveries,' expressed great trust not only in the healing of her daughter, but in the validity of the Medjugorje apparitions."*[2]

For critics and skeptics, there was obviously plenty of room for ridicule and denunciation of Linda's "faith-driven" comments. Indeed, Audrey's mother can easily be castigated for declaring that God was at work in the life of her daughter. And it can be argued that Linda was only a hopeful mother who was desperately searching for something good to come out of such a terrible tragedy.

But for people who understand the profound and intricate nature of deep faith, there is no mystery. Such a faith transcends desperate hope. It is akin to a special window which allows us to see into the ways of God. Indeed, Linda's suspicions and her subsequent public assertions were built upon a truth surrounding Audrey that perhaps God was choosing to reveal to only a few at the time, especially Linda. And with this possibility, through the eyes of faith, the entire series of events and Linda's own actions become a path of logical steps in God's plan to lead the faithful to do His will.

Religious history shows that this has happened many times before. Indeed, when divinely inspired and orchestrated situations begin to arise, the great saints and mystics note that it is only through the response of the faithful that God's plan can be fulfilled. Therefore, Linda's interpretations of the events surrounding her daughter and her own public witness could either be wholeheartedly dismissed, or they could be viewed as possibly having some purpose, a divinely-inspired purpose. But even so, those with weak faith would surely demand more to convince them of this truth.

Fortunately, in such circumstances the *truth* is usually revealed if God is truly at work. For in these cases, God goes "overboard", preparing a careful plan not for those strong in faith, but rather for

His lost and disinterested sheep. This plan forms a step-by-step process for bringing souls home, a loving nurturing of souls that need just the right amount of attention and prompting to be reawakened and healed.

And indeed, by the time Linda began to express her inclinations, it appeared that God *was* also advancing Audrey's story in a most formidable fashion. In retrospect, the mystery surrounding the life and tragic accident of Audrey Santo was slowly moving to a higher level. And soon, several more pieces of the puzzle began to come together. Time would show that these pieces were, indeed, important.

As mentioned, there was a great outpouring of prayer for Audrey from the very beginning. However, soon a reverse phenomenon began to slowly reveal itself. Not surprisingly, it appears that this phenomenon actually began around the same time that the Spirit was moving Linda so overtly.

According to the family, several people who visited Audrey began to declare that they were asking Audrey to pray for them. Then, in November of 1987, one man reported that he had said to Audrey, *"Pray for me, Audrey."* And he did so under the understanding that Audrey showed no sign of being able to hear, much less respond to such a request. Likewise, similar remarks began to come from people who visited Audrey. Other visitors began to report being touched in a special way by her. Curiously, some said that they smelled roses in her presence. Most amazing, however, were certain dramatic spiritual awakenings suddenly being attributed to encounters with the suffering child.

Although illogical and undefinable, the number of these types of reports gradually grew. At the same time, well-wishers and people of all faiths continued to pour into the Santo home to visit Audrey. And by now, it appeared that people were being inspired to help Audrey in many profound ways .

Over and over, visitors would bring gifts to hopefully induce a spiritual healing for Audrey. Some brought prayer cards and Mass cards; others would bring holy relics, medals, sacred pictures and blessed icons from all over the world. Some brought the healing water of Lourdes, while others brought oils known for miraculous cures and recoveries. Even the famous traveling Pilgrim Virgin of

Fatima statue came to the Santo home.

Then, a Friday night "Rosary group" formed and began to meet just to pray for Audrey. At first, there was only a handful of people. But gradually, hundreds started to come. Jeri Cox said about it all: "I found it really overwhelming. People have come and God's brought so many people to prayer through Audrey. I've seen so much happen through Audrey. I have seen a small prayer group grow into hundreds of people on a Friday night. Audrey's just drawn people to herself."

Most significantly, as these well-wishers (among them many religious leaders) departed, they would note that they felt"touched" in a special way by Audrey. It was something they couldn't understand, they said, but it transcended mere *"feelings"*. And even though they had come for Audrey's healing, some were beginning to report that they were receiving healing, as ailments and infirmities were *"vanishing"*. Likewise, a few people openly declared that they had *"come not just to pray for Audrey, but to pray with Audrey."* Some people would even *"ask"* for Audrey's "blessing".

Once more, these reports were matters of faith. But like Linda's declarations, they can be recognized as inspirations of the Spirit, as they had to be seen and understood with the soul, not the mind. Indeed, Audrey Santo's life was apparently becoming a source for unity and healing, and this mystery was only in its earliest stages.

But in August of 1988, just weeks after Linda and Audrey returned from Medjugorje, it wasn't what was *vanishing* that created a great stir, but rather what appeared.

As Dr. Riordan began his regular examination of Audrey, he was suddenly taken back. There, in the center of Audrey's palm, was a red excoriation mark. Seconds later, the puzzled doctor noticed that the same kind of red mark had appeared on Audrey's other palm, and no one could figure out why.

It was a significant moment. And those closest to Audrey started to see that what they had been saying all along about the suffering child was perhaps more true than even they realized.

Yes, Audrey Santo was proving to be special, special beyond everyone's greatest imagination. And maybe, just maybe, many of the startling declarations concerning Audrey were not so crazy after all.

CHAPTER THIRTEEN

"WHAT ARE YOU DOING, AUDREY?"

"What are you doing, Audrey?" the befuddled doctor muttered, half to himself and half to Audrey, as he struggled to make sense from what he was observing.

The scenario was baffling. In routine weekly examinations of Audrey's entire body, little red excoriation marks would suddenly appear and then disappear in the center of her palms. Sometimes this mystery occurred on just one hand, sometimes on the other hand, and sometimes on both. Often, Audrey's doctor did a "double take" as before he knew it, the marks would apparently vanish into thin air.

In nine years (1987-1996), Audrey Santo has never exhibited a bedsore or redness on her body of any kind. But just weeks after returning home from Medjugorje, the little red marks on her hands repeatedly appeared and disappeared. Without question, no one knew what to make of it.

"It started to happen all the time," said Linda. "The doctor would see the mark on the right hand and then on the other hand. Then they would be gone. It looked like an excoriation. But Audrey didn't get a hole in her hands. The red marks would just appear and disappear on her hands."

Then, one September morning in 1988, a nurse named Martha

became extremely animated over what she discovered on Audrey's body.

Responding to Martha's concerns, Linda raced into Audrey's room to see what was the matter. At once, Martha carefully showed Linda several "stripe marks" which appeared across the front of Audrey's body.

The marks looked like purple and red streaks, or thin welts. They stretched over Audrey's face, shoulders, arms, stomach and legs. From head to toe, it appeared as if someone had scourged the child.

"It looked like someone hit her with a belt or something thin like a tube," recalled Linda in an attempt to describe the newest development. "There were streaky marks all over the anterior portion of Audrey's body. It looked like she was 'whipped'."

The strange marks not only came out of nowhere and covered Audrey's whole body, but they departed just as quickly, as if by-passing the normal stages of healing for such lacerations. Linda said, "Whatever happened, the marks vanished so completely that there was absolutely no period of time for healing. They just disappeared."

The repeated manifestations became mind-boggling for the doctors and nurses. To put it bluntly, upon repeated examinations of the mysterious marks and stripes, the doctors "were losing it," Linda said.

The reason for their reaction was simple. No clinical explanation for what was occurring could be offered. Although Audrey had received an insult to the brain from her accident, the fact that she never displayed any seizures or changes in her bodily functions now complicated the matter. Simply stated, the doctors were inclined to believe that these "strange marks" were not coming from an injured brain.

In October of 1988, the phenomenon of the red marks on Audrey's hands repeated itself and was consistently documented. By this time, the marks were very evident and would last for days. Records indicate that on October 26, 1988, cavities formed within Audrey's hands without medical reason. The holes then disappeared on October 29th, only to reappear with more depth on October 31st.

In addition, strange dove-like images began to appear and protrude on the outside upper portion of Audrey's hands. These images would stick out from the surface of her skin on both hands. Like the red marks on her hands, they would then disappear.

Around this time, Audrey also began to exhibit what is known as the "phenomenon of weight". To put it simply, for no apparent reason Audrey's body became impossible to lift or move. This little child, who was just four-years-old and weighed less than thirty pounds, would suddenly arch her back into a fixed position that would leave her literally unmovable.

Simultaneously with the assumed position, Audrey's pulse would suddenly elevate from a normal pulse of 80-90 beats per minute to 185-200. This phenomenon would then last for as long as eight continuous hours, which is considered medically impossible to survive. It is a physical phenomenon only known to occur when a visionary or mystic is believed to be in an altered state of consciousness.

"There was no responding to anything," explained Linda regarding Audrey's dead weight and rapid pulse. "Audrey's eyes would be open, but she wouldn't respond to anything. And we couldn't move her. She was too heavy. It appeared like she was in what mystical theologians call ecstasy."

In January of 1989, Audrey's right foot exhibited the same type of red marks that had been found on her hands. After this, Linda now began to suspect that what Audrey was experiencing was not physical in origin. Rather, the marks appeared to be mystical in nature.

Others agreed. Perhaps God was at work in this child in a very confusing and, for some, very frightening manner. For just as certain saints and mystics before her, it seemed that Audrey's body was exhibiting the Sacred Stigmata of Jesus Christ.

But, since Audrey was unable to communicate, it was only possible to hypothesize about the nature of the bizarre events surrounding the physical manifestations on her body.

Then, during the 1989 Lenten season, the strange events began to occur in clusters. And along with all the marks on Audrey's body, something else became apparent: *Audrey was experiencing intense pain and suffering.* Her agony even grew to the point where she required hospitalization, yet nothing pathological or dysfunctional was diagnosed.

Finally, during Holy Week of the same Lenten season, Audrey's crying and suffering became almost unbearable for the family and staff to watch. Yet suddenly, at three o'clock on Good Friday, her agony completely stopped and she fell into a deep sleep.

Because of all of this, there now existed a new kind of stress for those caring for or visiting Audrey. For with each such episode, suspicions grew stronger and stronger.

Little Audrey Santo, almost all those closest to her suspected, was being called and used by the Lord as an instrument in His plan of salvation. And if this were so, it meant that Grandma Nader's words concerning her precious granddaughter were more true than even she suspected.

Indeed, Audrey appeared to be truly *"chosen"*.

CHAPTER FOURTEEN

IMITATING CHRIST

For hundreds of years, scientists and mystical theologians have studied individuals who have apparently exhibited the stigmata of Christ. But what exactly is the meaning of this phenomenon? And who are those individuals who seemingly carry Christ's wounds in their bodies?

From a purely objective standpoint, theologians classify such experiences as "psycho-physiological" phenomena. These phenomena consist of levitation, luminous rays, fragrant odors, prolonged fasting and stigmatization.

Specifically, psycho-physiological phenomena seem to directly affect a human being's body, but they are less related to so-called "ecstasy". Rationalists attempt to explain these phenomena by natural causes. This amounts to saying that their own scientific model has failed to produce a definitive answer, and they cannot offer a sufficient explanation.

But in view of the fact that some alleged reports of psycho-physiological phenomena have been successfully proven to have purely biological or physical causes, rationalists are satisfied to argue that all such phenomena can be explained away as "mind-power", psychological tricks, or deception.

However, it is no secret that most psycho-physiological phenomena have been found to be directly related to individuals who demonstrate lives of great virtue, sanctity and piousness. And with this bit of historical knowledge, those with faith can confidently believe what they already suspect is the truth: God is truly behind such unexplainable events as the stigmata, and through such phenomena, He is speaking to His people and trying to help them to know Him better through both faith and reason.

Moreover, theologians say that stigmatists are intended by God as beacons of His light and His truth for all to see. Mr. Michael Freze, S.F.O., in his book, *They Bore The Wounds of Christ,* succinctly sums up one of the most incredible mysteries of the Christian faith - the stigmata. Wrote Mr. Freze:

> Despite the rich deposit Sacred Tradition has left to us, some mysteries of the faith continue to fascinate and even baffle the best of minds, be they theologians or lay persons. Such is the case with a mystical phenomenon known as the Sacred Stigmata...[1]

The rich legacy of the stigmata is said to have begun with St. Paul, while St. Francis of Assisi is probably the most famous stigmatist.

According to the renowned Parisian scholar, Dr. Imbert-Gourbeyre, there have been 321 authentic stigmatists in Church history. This particular list was compiled in 1984. In his monumental two-volume work, *La Stigmatization,* Dr. Gourbeyre identifies sixty-two stigmatists who have been canonized or beatified by the Church.

According to Mr. Freze, the twentieth century may rightly be called the "era of the stigmatist", since more than two dozen cases of stigmatization have been reported and investigated. However, few have been authenticated by the proper Church authorities. But unlike past centuries, noted Mr. Freze, there are now thoroughly-documented cases of many living and recently deceased stigmatists who have undergone extensive investigations by both medical experts and theologians.[2]

Mr. Freze also pointed out that significant evidence from the world of photography, anatomy, biology and chemistry helps to substantiate these claims.

Because of this evidence, the question of authentic stigmatization is now more than a theological curiosity. It is an observable fact. While still a rare phenomenon, the Sacred Stigmata is truly one of the greatest miracles known to Christendom, especially considering that there are over one billion Christians in the world. Indeed, it is perhaps the greatest visible sign of Christ's presence among us today.[3] Wrote Mr. Freze:

It's as though Our Lord still shows mercy to the "Doubting Thomases" of our world by allowing them to be witnesses to the reality of God in our midst. **"Put your finger here and see My Hands, and put out your hand and place it in My Side. Do not be faithless, but believe"**. (Jn 20:27) Without a doubt, God has gifted us today with a sign of the times, a sign displayed through victim souls known as stigmatists. These souls share in the sufferings of Our Lord's Passion to redeem the world. These are extraordinary souls, holy and pure. By imitating Christ so intensely, they have been invited to become one with Him. They are His beloved. He demands much from their example and from their sacrifice. Those imprinted with Our Lord's wounds upon their bodies become transformed into living crucifixes by sharing in His Passion for the redemption of the world. They are His most chosen souls.[4]

With all of this in mind, we come face to face with the profound depth of the reality of Grandma Nader's humble words. For if the physical manifestations on little Audrey's hands and feet, as well as her entire body, were mystical in nature, and if she were truly beginning to exhibit the Sacred Stigmata, then Audrey was now one of those whom Mr. Freze wrote about so poignantly. In God's eyes, Audrey had been chosen to be *"one with in Him"*, and she was called to expiate for sins in union with the Lord. Therefore, little Audrey Santo was now perhaps among the "chosen of the chosen".

Throughout history, such chosen souls have usually provided a wealth of information through the conduct of their lives, as well as through their words, thus helping the faithful accept that God has truly chosen them.

Through the stigmatist's words and actions, and not just through his wounds, the faithful are especially called to the truth about the gift the soul has received. Indeed, the details of the stigmatist's entire life determine his authenticity to some degree. They also sometimes reveal the reason why this "chosen" soul is worthy of such grace.

However, each and every case is different. No two chosen souls have ever lived identical lives or exhibited identical experiences. There is always variation in one form or another, whether it be the exact location of the stigmata on their hands or wrists, or in the revelations they bring through their lives and experiences. Furthermore, each chosen soul has a unique mission.

But, in discerning the unexplainable events surrounding little Audrey, we are left in wonder and awe. As Audrey is a child and she cannot physically speak, we are unable to fully explore her life in every detail. Therefore, with Audrey, God seems to be inviting us into the very depths of a mystery. And perhaps, only those with great faith will be able to accept this mystery.

With her faith always deep and alive in her heart, Linda Santo suspected that Audrey had been chosen. For Linda, it was apparent; the evidence was mounting daily. The doctors had told Linda that the unexplainable marks on Audrey's body offered no scientific explanation. And considering their nature, these markings bore a direct resemblance to those previously discovered on known stigmatists.

Simply put, the marks weren't just random and red; rather they were open holes that bled on the palms of Audrey's hands and on the anterior surface of her foot. Likewise, the stripes looked exactly like whip marks. Furthermore, Audrey was obviously in great pain. Apparently, then, everything added up to something very serious. But how could the Santo Family know for sure if Audrey was truly experiencing the Sacred Stigmata?

To abolish some of the family's confusion, in 1989 a new set of circumstances came into play during Holy Week (the pinnacle of the Christian calendar when Jesus' crucifixion, death and resurrection are remembered).

Audrey's physical manifestations and sufferings began to show themselves in a way and at a time that seemed directly related to the life and death of Jesus Christ. And since Audrey was in a coma-like state, and since she was only a child with no historical knowledge of the important Christian celebrations during that time of the year, the only logical conclusion was indeed mystical — particularly in light of the fact that, throughout history during the Easter season, stigmatists have suffered in this manner.

While she had not kept exact records of Holy Week 1989 as methodically as later years, Linda remembered the details quite well:

> Audrey suffered a lot that Lent. We were trying to figure out what was wrong with her. She was in such pain. She was crying and in pain. We're talking copious amounts of tears. Her face was red and she would be sobbing. There were also constant red marks on Audrey's hands and then they would disappear completely. After that it just escalated.

Yes, as incredible as it all was, the mystical events surrounding the life of little Audrey Santo began to escalate. For not long after that Easter, a shower of signs and wonders descended upon the Santo home almost as if to emphasize the great prodigy which was occurring in Audrey's life.

In fact, so many miraculous events began occurring that it seemed as if Heaven was determined to compensate for Audrey's silence and to firmly establish that she had been called by God for an extraordinary mission.

CHAPTER FIFTEEN

SIGNS AND WONDERS

Even before the trip to Medjugorje, Linda seemed led by the Holy Spirit to proclaim that her daughter's coma-like existence held a special meaning.

Over and over, Linda repeated her beliefs. God was *"using Audrey"* and He *"had a plan for her life."* Yet, although Linda believed in her heart that this was true, she struggled to identify exactly *how* God's plan in Audrey's life was manifesting itself.

But when Audrey appeared to exhibit physical manifestations of the stigmata and other mystical sufferings, even Linda was taken aback. For she had not anticipated such incredible happenings, nor did she suspect what was yet to come.

And indeed, much more soon unfolded.

During the time when Audrey's body began to reveal the red, sometimes bleeding, marks on her hands and feet and other apparent signs of mystical suffering, the family simultaneously began to observe some strange happenings.

Throughout the Santo home, curious little oddities began to occur, such as religious statues turning color or seeming to move, or the sudden scent of roses coming from out of nowhere.

In Audrey's room, where Bishop Bernard Flanagan of the Worcester Diocese had granted permission for a tabernacle with consecrated Communion hosts to be placed, nurses reported during

78

shift changes that some of the statues in the room were somehow *"turning and facing"* the tabernacle. These bizarre happenings would repeatedly occur, even though the statues were constantly repositioned away from the tabernacle. When questioned, nurses and family members vehemently denied that they had turned the statues. On top of that, rosaries and chaplets were suddenly turning gold. And holy water, when touched to Audrey, would somehow glitter and sparkle in an extraordinary way.

Then another strange activity began to develop before the nurses' and family's startled eyes. For some totally inexplicable reason, Audrey's mechanical respirator and feeding tube would periodically stop. Upon investigation, no defects could be found in the operation of the equipment. Attorney Dan Lynch of Vermont wrote of this phenomenon in his December 1996 newsletter, *The Herald of the Reign of the Queen.* Mr. Lynch wrote:

> Audrey has baffled medical science by different phenomena. She can stop her mechanical respirator from working and she can stop the flow of her feeding tube to her stomach. The latter is called "Audrey's fasting". The feeding tube automatically feeds Audrey's stomach liquid food by gravity and it is "impossible" to stop it. But when Audrey fasts, it stops.

Audrey's mother said that, once again, this was another mystery that totally confounded the doctors. "It just stops somehow," said Linda, "it's incredible. Yet, she doesn't lose any weight. The doctors and nurses were blown away. Now, they accept it."

At the time, the Santo family believed that many of these inexplicable events were little signs that Audrey was going to be healed. "Things started to happen," said Linda. "But our excitement was not in what was happening. Our excitement was that these were signs from God saying, 'Yes, Audrey would be healed.' That's what we were looking for — her healing."

But after Easter of 1989, the supernatural events in the Santo home began to multiply. Indeed, it appears that God's plan for this child continued to unfold. And the number and variety of signs and wonders that were a part of it seemed unlimited.

"Signs, wonders and miracles — yes! Sensationalism — no!"[1]

This is what one noted author on supernatural matters once wrote in order to admonish the skeptics. He noted how God is often accused, even by those looked upon as spiritual leaders, of being unwise or haphazard in granting signs to His people.

Undoubtedly, these voices of concern often speak out in good conscience. However, perhaps they fail to recognize how weak faith is in today's world, just as Our Lady stated in her early apparitions at Medjugorje. Indeed, although the faithful need to be prudent and cautious in their judgment, to refuse to even look is foolish and truly unwise.

In both the Old and New Testaments, God granted many signs and wonders for the good of His people. Over the centuries, it has remained this way. Our Creator often works numerous miracles, cures and wonders to alert spiritually-minded people. These signs are clear declarations of His love, and not merely circus thrills or entertainment.

Most significantly, signs and wonders are quite often signals which seek to trigger a reaction from a sinful and unrepentant world. They call us to God's mercy, as His divine patience forestalls His justice. Experts say that God designs these actions to strike in a formidable way at human consciences in order to lead His people from the "darkness."

Through wisdom, a soul can retain the duty to recognize such signs and wonders, for they are light, they are truth and **"the truth shall set you free"** (Jn 8:32). Indeed, Scripture also assures, **"He who acts in truth comes into the light"** (Jn 3:21).

Thus, those with a sincere heart must then realize that God's signs and wonders are not sensationalism, but rather invitations to discern His call through prayer.

But, what is God saying during our present times? For according to many experts, never before has the world experienced so many signs and wonders. Perhaps Archbishop George Pearce, S.M., said it best in his forward to a book entitled *Signs and Wonders*:

"Of recent years, God has outdone Himself, as it were in multiplying the signs of His presence among us in an endless number of ways. And He has even provided us with signs which point to the

signs."[2]

Archbishop Pearce's words could not be more true. At Fatima on October 13, 1917, over 70,000 witnesses watched the sun spin, dance and then plunge toward the earth. This was the "sign" promised by the Virgin Mary to the three visionaries on July 13, 1917 in order to prove that she was truly appearing at Fatima. Later, Pope Paul VI would declare in his encyclical, *Signum Magnum,* that Mary was *"the Great Sign"*.

At Medjugorje, it has been the same. The twirling sun giving off a kaleidoscope of colors, the spinning illuminated cross on Mt. Krizevac, and many more such phenomena have all been signs of the real sign — Mary. And Mary is none other than the great sign whose only goal is to point to her son, Jesus.

Moreover, today's signs truly do point to more signs, and hopefully to what God is trying to convey. We are called to recognize God's presence and power in these events. And these events then often point to the words of His prophets.

Over the centuries, God's hand could be recognized in the holy lives and the prophetic preaching of many great saints and chosen ones, whose lives have often been marked by unusual signs and miracles. From the Sacred Stigmata to the "incorruption" of their deceased bodies, extraordinary wonders have often accompanied holy lives. Once again, these signs again point to more signs, as the very existence of these great souls becomes a special invitation to us from God to listen and learn from them.

In the events surrounding little Audrey Santo, we are again confronted with these mysteries. For although Audrey's life itself is a sign of God's presence in a special way, the numerous miracles and phenomena that emerged at the Santo home soon began to point to this chosen soul's mission, one apparently designed to bring unity, healing and peace to God's people through their Savior, Jesus Christ.

Blood. Tears. Oil. Mysterious odors and scents. Over the previous seven years (1989-1996), the Santo family home has become a mystical wonderland of heavenly gifts and mysterious intercessions.

From 1989 to 1992, a generous number of miracles occurred in the home. But beginning in 1993, an extraordinary number of new phenomena materialized.

It all began when an image of Our Lady of Guadalupe resting on a piano in the Santo home began weeping tears of oil at 1 p.m. on October 28, 1993. The image had been given to Audrey by the Apostolate of the Missionary Image of Our Lady of Guadalupe, which escorts a four-foot by six-foot photographic replica of the original tilma of Our Lady of Guadalupe throughout the world.

Since June 14, 1991, the Missionary Image of Our Lady of Guadalupe has traveled throughout America in order to "melt hearts" and "bring conversion", just as Our Lady of Guadalupe originally did for over nine million peasant Indians in the sixteenth century. Most significantly, the Missionary Image of Our Lady of Guadalupe travels on a moral mission intended to supernaturally aid in the efforts to end the evil of abortion, and to help the forces of life defeat the "culture of death".

Over the years, the Missionary Image's path has left a trail of miracles, enough to fill more than a few books. Then, when it was brought into the Santo home on August 9, 1994, for the very first time the Missionary Image itself began to profusely weep tears of oil, like the smaller image of Our Lady of Guadalupe. It was an incredible sign that certainly once again pointed to the suffering Audrey and her mission in Christ.

Sonia Huerta, R.N., one of the nurses at the Santo home at the time of the first miracle, remembered that it was like watching a person cry. "She was sobbing tears and tears. I couldn't believe what I was seeing," recalled Sonia. "I didn't know what to do... It was just exuding oil, incredible amounts of oil... There were gauzes all saturated with oil. The dish was full of oil too. And the fragrance was wonderful."[3] Fr. Emmanuel also recalled the first Guadalupe image which wept oil in the Santo home. "I remember there was a very distinct smell of roses," he said, "I have sinus problems and haven't smelled roses in thirty years or so. It was like when I smelled roses in my childhood."

Then, not long afterward, a gallery of icons, pictures and statues in the Santo home began to cry tears or shed oil. From a picture of St. Rita of Lebanon which wept tears of blood, to a Rosa Mystica statue which shed real tears, supernatural events of this nature started to occur almost daily.

Of course, all this was so overwhelming that no one knew what to expect next. For just when everyone thought they had seen it all, something even more incredible occurred right before their startled eyes.

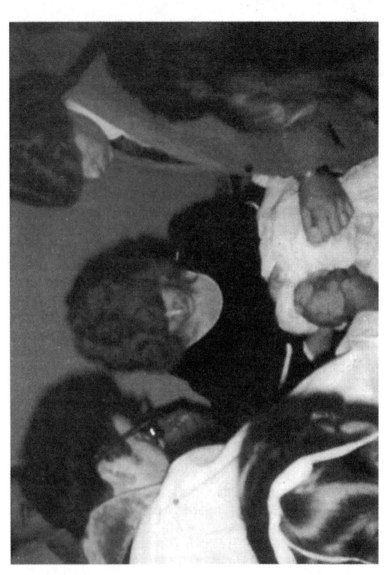

Fr. Leo Barry baptizes Audrey

Audrey and Stephen, not long before the accident.

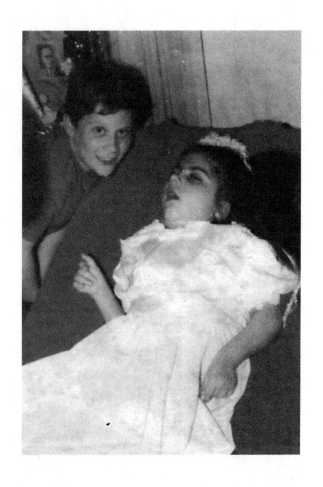

Stephen, age ten, with Audrey, age eight.

Matthew Santo and Stephen Sr.

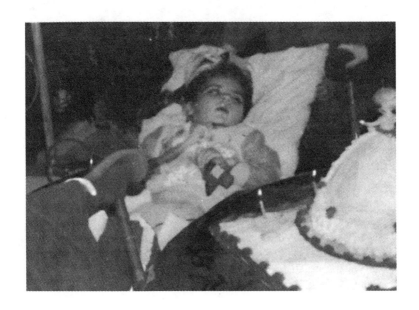

Audrey's fourth birthday
December 19, 1989

Audrey with Missionary
Image of Guadelupe

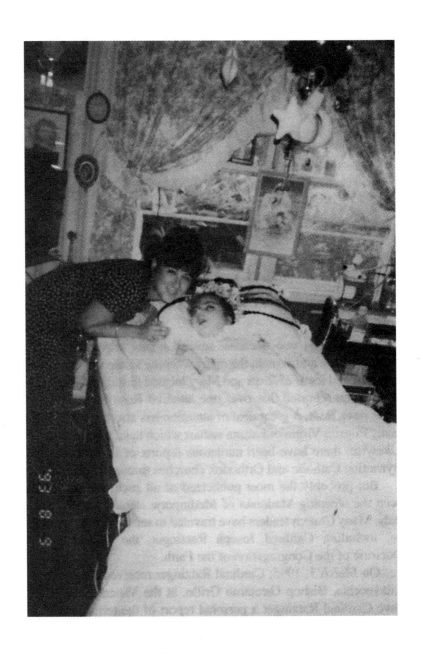

Audrey with her sister, Jennifer

CHAPTER SIXTEEN

"THE VERY HEAVENS ARE WEEPING"

Over the last two decades, several books have attempted to chronicle and explain the many weeping statues, pictures, photographs and icons of Jesus and Mary located throughout the world. It has been reported that over one hundred Rosa Mystica statues alone have wept. A great deal of attention has also been paid to the many Pilgrim Virgin of Fatima statues which have reportedly cried. Likewise, there have been numerous reports of icons weeping in Byzantine Catholic and Orthodox churches throughout the world.

But probably the most publicized of all such phenomena has been the weeping Madonna of Medjugorje statue in Citavecchia, Italy. Many Church leaders have traveled to see the miraculous statue, including Cardinal Joseph Ratzinger, the Prefect for the Doctrine of the Congregation of the Faith.

On March 1, 1995, Cardinal Ratzinger received the Bishop of Citavecchia, Bishop Girotamo Grillo, at the Vatican. The bishop gave Cardinal Ratzinger a personal report of the terra-cotta statue of the Virgin Mary of Medjugorje that has been weeping tears of blood. According to the periodical, *Inside the Vatican*, the news had so rocked Italy that the Holy See decided to learn more about the phenomenon.

But this specific report involved just one weeping statue, as similar phenomena usually do. Occasionally, a report may concern more than one statue or picture, but this is rare.

Rare, that is, except in the Santo home.

Over the last several years, literally dozens of statues, pictures, paintings, photographs, postcards and icons have wept there, which is "extraordinary" even to the experts.

From the fall of 1993 until the summer of 1995, the following miraculous events were reported in the Santo home:

1) - on November 3, 1993, during Holy Mass in Audrey's room, the image of Our Lady of Guadalupe again exuded oil;

2) - on November 5, 1993, a statue of Our Lady of Lourdes wept tears from its right eye and emitted the scent of roses;

3) - on November 9, 1993, a Head of Christ statue exuded oil accompanied by the scent of roses;

4) - on November 11, 1993, a San Damiano Cross exuded oil from the left side;

5) - on Christmas Day, December 25, 1993, an image of the Christ Child holding the world exuded oil;

6) - on December 29, 1993, a Pieta statue shed oil;

7) - on December 29, 1993, a Rosa Mystica statue shed salty tears;

8) - on December 29, 1993, a Saint Michael statue shed oil;

9) - on December 29, 1993, a white alabaster Head of Christ statue shed oil;

10) - on December 29, 1993, an image of Holy Jesus shed oil;

11) - on December 31, 1993, a small picture of the Head of Christ shed oil;

12) - on January 8, 1994, a picture of the Face of Christ over the tabernacle shed oil;

13) - on January 8, 1994, an Our Lady of the Americas statue shed oil;

14) - on January 8, 1994, a twelve-inch statue of the Sacred Heart of Jesus shed oil;

15) - on January 8, 1994, the odor of sweet wine was detected in Audrey's room;

16) - on January 8, 1994, a picture of the Head of Christ from the Last Vision of Sr. Lucia of Fatima shed oil;

17) - on January 21, 1994, a statue of Our Lady of the Americas shed oil from its left eye;

18) - on January 27, 1994, a twelve-inch statue of the Sacred Heart shed oil; there was also the odor of sweet wine;

19) - on February 16, 1994, a large crucifix shed oil from the body of Christ; there was also the fragrance of vinegar;

20) - on February 23, 1994, three different crucifixes of various sizes shed oil;

21) - on March 4, 1994, a picture of the Head of Christ shed oil;

22) - on March 13, 1994, a solid gold crucifix shed oil;

23) - on March 17, 1994, an Infant Child of Prague statue shed oil;

24) - on April 23, 1994, a statue of the Baby Jesus in a wooden manger shed tears of oil;

25) - on May 9, 1994, an Our Lady of Lourdes statue shed a darker colored oil;

26) - on July 31, 1994, a statue of Our Lady of Mt. Carmel shed oil from its crown;

27) - on July 31, 1994, a picture of Our Lady of Mt. Carmel shed oil;

28) - on July 31, 1994 a picture of the Christ Child in Mary's hand shed oil;

29) - on September 23, 1994, a statue of the Good Shepherd shed oil from the left eye;

30) - on October 30, 1994, a statue of the Good Shepherd shed blood down the left side of its face onto Christ's gown. Two red dots were also found on the forehead of Christ;

31) - on October 13, 1994, a Head of Christ statue shed blood from its left eye;

32) - on December 13, 1994, a Rosa Mystica statue shed blood down its left cheek;

33) - on January 18, 1995, a large Sacred Heart statue shed oil;

34) - on March 7, 1995, an Our Lady of Czestochowa icon shed oil from its left eye;

35) - on March 14, 1995, a Rosa Mystica statue shed oil from its left eye;

36) - on April 16 (Easter Sunday), 1995, two full-sized angel statues shed oil from their heads;

37) - on July 17, 1995, a Christ the King statue shed blood;

38) - on July 17, 1995, a Good Shepherd statue shed blood.

Since July of 1995, there have been many more of these kinds of reports, indicating that the phenomena are not slowing down. "Week after week," said Fr. George V. Joyce, one of Audrey's spiritual directors, "statues and paintings and images are weeping oil. And then we saw a number of them started to weep blood."

In a home where the walls in several rooms are literally plastered with statues, pictures, paintings, icons and crucifixes, the Santo family never knew what to expect next. Truly, the home had become an oasis of the supernatural. And these incredible events weren't confined to the inside of the house. On July 6, 1997, two angels placed in a bird bath in front of Audrey's window in the front yard shed oil from their eyes.

But as prudence would dictate, Audrey's spiritual directors approached this overwhelming yet puzzling scenario with great caution. Concerning all the incredible phenomena, Fr. Emmanuel explained, "After the Guadalupe painting shed oil, I went up to the Santo house to carefully see for myself what was reported. With the Guadalupe painting and all the phenomena, I have always looked for fraud. But I have not found a scintilla of evidence that there is fraud going on."

Considering the nature of these events, the tendency to make accusations is likely, but Fr. Emmanuel cautioned that onlookers need to be very careful. Said Fr. Emmanuel:

"Until you have the proof of fraud, the only position you should have is silent seeking. The Church says that you don't have to believe in any of this. It's all private revelation. However, basic human decency, fairness and justice require that until you explicitly have concrete evidence of fraud - you refrain from all innuendo that there is fraud. I never stop looking for fraud. I have to be objective. Everything I personally talk about when I speak about Audrey has nothing to do with the physical manifestations. People can dismiss the paranormal. What people cannot dismiss is the truth about God, suffering, evil, and Jesus's love and care for humanity that is being revealed through the life of Audrey and the Santo family."

Not surprisingly, the Santo family had their own concerns about what some people might think. As Linda Santo had such strong faith in God as a *"God of miracles"*, her outspokenness in declaring that He was working in Audrey, along with her public statements concerning the apparitions of the Virgin Mary in Medjugorje, gave plenty of ammunition to anyone wanting to accuse her of affecting this remarkable situation. But again, Fr. Emmanuel was adamant that no such manipulation was at hand in Audrey's case. After years of observing the events surrounding the child, Fr. Emmanuel said:

> Linda was really worried when all this started. But she bears no responsibility for it. She didn't bring it about. There is a difference being a very pivotal character in God's plan and someone trying to orchestrate it. Linda's subjective experiences, especially with mystical phenomena, is intense. But her time with Audrey, her care for Audrey is what she is all about. God works through simple, limited, faithful people, which Linda is. Under no circumstances has she ever lied to me about the abnormal physical phenomena. God does not need one lie, one sin, to fully accomplish all he wants to accomplish. In fact, Linda's subjective reaction to all of the phenomena is irrelevant. What is very relevant for me is the care Audrey receives, not the phenomena surrounding her. Linda is doing the little deeds of love well. The power here is that there are little people doing extraordinary things in Christ. And they are doing them by living in extraordinary fidelity to the way of Jesus.

Since October of 1994, more than three dozen images in the chapel and Audrey's room have shed oil or blood. Some of them exuded so much oil that little bowls had to be placed under them to collect it all. Laboratory analysis of the oil revealed some of it to be "olive oil". But the composition of the other samples was determined to be "unknown".

Dr. Boguslaw Lipinski, Ph.D., noted in the Mercy Foundation's documentary, *Audrey's Life*, that this was something very unexpected. He stated for the record that the chemical analysis of the oils did not reveal any characteristics of the known edible oils. But it was certainly a vegetative or natural oil. However, Lipinski confessed, *"we do not know exactly...what."*[1]

What, then, are we to make of all these weeping, shedding and bleeding manifestations, besides the fact that they point to Audrey's mission in Christ? What is the profound meaning of these phenomena? What, if anything, is God trying to tell us?

Experts say that the sadness and sorrow of Christ and His mother express through various weeping images and other phenomena seem to reinforce the message of various modern apparitions, prophecies and warnings. Many believe that these events are part of an era of heavenly warnings that began at Rue du Bac, Paris in 1830 with the apparitions of the Virgin Mary to St. Catherine Labouré, which were then confirmed and continued in the 1917 apparitions of the Virgin Mary at Fatima.

Indeed, the very number of weeping and bleeding statues, pictures and icons since 1981 constitutes a great sign of the times. Throughout the world, there has been an incredible array of such images weeping tears, oil and blood.

As oil is traditionally recognized as a sign of healing, reconciliation and salvation, and blood is a sign of life, the weeping images in the Santo family home must bear this same significance. Fr. Albert Hebert, an expert in such phenomena, wrote the following regarding what the many signs may be meant to tell us:

> Many persons have already formed their own conclusions. We simply say here that Christ and Mary and the very heavens are weeping over the vast amount of evil and sin in the world which threaten the Church and all mankind. Christ and Mary weep also over the sufferings of the good and innocent, particularly over the aborted babies and scandal given to the young. They suffer mystically in all the sufferings of the Mystical Body of Christ. But the weeping and bleeding images alone should be enough to bring men to conversion and repentance. The very wood, plaster and stone about us cry out![2]

Many experts have echoed Fr. Hebert's words. However, the best source to explain the meaning of these heavenly manifestations is perhaps Our Lady herself.

In a 1995 message to Fr. Stefano Gobbi of Italy, the Virgin Mary revealed why so many of her images are crying throughout the world. This message later received an Imprimatur from Cardinal Bernardino Echeverria Ruiz, O.F.M., of Ecuador. Mary said:

The time has come when I will make myself more manifest in the Church, through increasingly greater signs.

My tears are shed in many places to call everyone back to the sorrowful Heart of their Mother. The tears of a mother succeed in moving the most hardened hearts. But now my tears, even tears of blood, leave many of my children completely indifferent. My messages will become all the more frequent, the more the voice of the ministers refuses to proclaim the truth. (October 30, 1975)[3]

But again, what are we to conclude about the phenomena surrounding little Audrey Santo in particular? For as she lays in her bed, literally dozens of statues and images in her home are weeping or shedding oil and blood. Fr. John Meade, another of Audrey's spiritual directors, said, "I think it is a plain sign from heaven that Our Lord is pointing out a masterpiece of His work and calling our attention to listen to Him and to be guided by Him."

Moreover, once again, these signs must be pointing to Audrey, a chosen soul apparently united with Christ in a mission to help our sinful world, to tell us something that perhaps many may not even see. Said Fr. Emmanuel:

If all people do is react and admire the phenomena, and do not act in their lives on the truth the Santo family has been chosen to communicate - which is intense, passionate, persevering care and concern for the littlest and the least, for the voiceless and for those suffering in silence - then the phenomena cannot serve the purpose for which God has granted them.

But even after the many miraculous manifestations, God still wasn't done in the Santo home. For after 1989, Audrey's mission became even more profound as both her suffering and the phenomena around her intensified.

Indeed, by 1992, Audrey's pain began to escalate in a way reminiscent of some of the great mystics of medieval times. And because of this, more and more people were becoming convinced: Little Audrey Santo truly appeared to be a *victim soul.*

CHAPTER SEVENTEEN

THE FULL PASSION

If there were winds of the supernatural blowing through the Santo home, in Audrey's bedroom, there was a full blown hurricane.

Joanne Erickson, a non-Catholic registered nurse, had taken care of Audrey for approximately three years. She wrote the following letter to one of Audrey's spiritual directors concerning her experiences in the Santo home and especially with Audrey.

Dear Fr. Sylvester,

I am writing as requested concerning Audrey Santo.

I have been with Audrey for nearly three years. Audrey is a beautiful child and very special to me.

I have seen statues and the chains of Rosaries change color. I have also seen the open creases in her palms, the marks on her left side and marks on her forehead. Audrey arches her head backward with eyes wide open and stares upward as if looking at something or someone. These episodes will last for a couple of minutes. She also goes into deep, coma-like sleeps when her skin looks wax-like and she becomes very cold to touch. There has also been the aroma of roses in her room and conversions which I am sure are due to the wonderful, religious atmosphere here. Many visitors have expressed a special feeling or "presence" when entering Audrey's room.

I pray you are in excellent health and look forward to seeing you again soon.

Sincerely,
Joanne Erickson[1]

Without question, there has been almost universal agreement that the many miracles are intended to be signs that point to Audrey and through Audrey to God. But when one profoundly contemplates the life of little Audrey, what one finds once more is the reality of her extreme suffering.

In fact, Audrey experienced so much suffering during Lent, especially Holy Week, of 1989, that a whole new reality began to emerge for her family. They now began to understand that if their little Audrey truly was a victim soul, then there were very serious implications to her suffering.

Indeed, Audrey appeared to be suffering in Christ, in union with His sufferings. Therefore, only by fully understanding how Christ suffered could the Santo family come to grips with what they were observing. For what was happening to their little girl was quite painful to watch. And to further complicate matters, the family still had to somehow recognize the difference between Audrey's mystical suffering and any suffering related to a true health problem.

Historically, this very difference has been difficult to discern with almost all mystics. However, these difficulties occurred with individuals who were able to communicate what they were experiencing. Audrey's silence obviously compounded the problem of determining exactly *when* and *what* was happening to her.

But ironically, her silence also provided a safe solution. As Audrey's mystical suffering was only accepted by the family and certain individuals of faith as an explanation for her various physical states, everything that Audrey experienced still had to be treated as if it were biological in nature, as this was the only safe course for her doctors and nurses to follow.

However, after Holy Week of 1989, the sheer intensity of what was happening with Audrey truly exploded. Even for her care providers, Audrey's mystical suffering became more and more extraordinary to observe and comprehend.

In the Mercy Foundation's documentary, *Audrey's Life*, one of Audrey's nurses, Sonia Huerta, R.N., discussed her observations of what Audrey would experience on Good Friday. Sonia said:

Noon would come and then all of a sudden her condition would change... All of a sudden she would get really agitated...her breathing would change, her respiratory rate would go really high up into the 50's sometimes. Her heart rate would increase up to 180, and it would last sometimes for hours... She would manifest signs of discomfort, like she was agonizing.

She would really get rigid at times, her body tone would change...her shoulders would go back and her chest would come forward. And her head would be all the way to the right... She would be breathing real fast... It was an intense time. No matter what you did for her, it wouldn't change her condition.[2]

In addition, Sonia also observed the stigmata on Audrey's body. She said she saw Audrey's palms get very red, raw and excoriated. She said Audrey's skin would peel, and all of a sudden sores on her palms would open up. Sonia also noted how the sores would just go away, and how this always occurred "during Lent."

Indeed, the Santo family and the nurses, too, began to now understand what it really meant for Audrey to be a victim soul. And fortunately, they were no longer alone in their belief, as the many priests who began to visit Audrey were often willing to voice their opinions.

Fr. Sylvester Catallo, an internationally-recognized expert on private revelations, stated after visiting Audrey, *"This child is truly a 'pure' victim soul. Many souls are saved through her suffering."* The Rev. Charles Babbit of Rhode Island declared that Audrey was *"a living saint"*. And one local diocesan priest stated that, *"Audrey has a mission of suffering for our sins as a continuation of Christ's crucifixion."*

Fr. Edward McDonough, of Boston believes that Audrey is a statement of life in a culture of death. Fr. McDonough said, *"In God's plan, her life is precious. He's using it. He's signifying the importance of life by the miracles that are surrounding it."* While Fr. John Meade, a local priest from Our Lady of Mt. Carmel, said,

"Audrey Santo is a tremendous treasure to our Church in this time in history. We need more victim souls, and she is serving so perfectly in her silent way."

Most impressively, one of the world's foremost experts in mystical phenomena, Fr. René Laurentin of France, visited Audrey and investigated the details of her case. Wrote Fr. Laurentin:

...through small daily signs of God's mysterious work, they truly live with the truth, those who have seized and understood one of these incomprehensible experiences which God has arisen today at this privileged place, this holy ground, for reparation of the sins of the world. Jesus is the one who first did this for us. He also invited His mother to share in His pain. Of this, Audrey and those who surround her are a living sign of this eternal mystery. What God has realized by her unfortunate circumstances, to be a source of healing for the world, we will only be able to understand fully in the life to come![3]

Fr. Laurentin's analysis and apparent acceptance of Audrey's victimhood compel us to ask many more questions. But the primary question is: How was all of this possible without the consent of Audrey's free will? For it is traditionally believed that victims in Christ do not have their victimhood forced upon them. Rather, they are permitted to choose if they wish to suffer in Christ.

Obviously, this question is impossible to answer since Audrey remains silent. Only God knows for sure. But perhaps, the answer has been forwarded.

According to one priest who visited her, Audrey Santo may have been given a choice in Medjugorje. During the brief moments in the apparition room and then, later when Audrey seemed to show some signs of recovery, she may have been asked of her own free will by God or Our Lady whether she wished to be healed or if she wished to *"offer herself to God as a victim soul."* This priest conjectured that she made "the heroic decision."

But according to Fr. Emmanuel, such a hypothetical possibility is unnecessary conjecture, because with her very baptism Audrey already consented for God to work in her in union with Christ. Therefore, any special circumstances at Medjugorje need not have occurred. Fr. Emmanuel said:

Audrey, by her baptism, is totally incorporated into Christ - baptism in Greek means total immersion - and therefore her life from that moment on is in Christ. Christ is more in her than she is in Christ. Therefore, after her baptism, every act of hers is moved out of the Spirit of Christ in whom she totally lives and moves and has her being. This, St. Paul made quite clear in Scripture.

For those who say Audrey gave no consent, they must understand her consent was in her baptism. The Gospel is clear - we don't choose Christ, Christ chooses us. John's Gospel tells us this. Under those circumstances, Jesus can choose Audrey for His purposes, which always includes suffering love.

To be baptized is to be baptized into Christ, it is to be baptized into the baptism he was baptized into. (Mk 10:38) It is to be baptized into Christ as sufferant servant. For when Jesus rises out of the waters at His baptism, He hears the words from heaven, **"This is my beloved Son, Whom I am well pleased,"** (Matt 3:17). These words are a direct reference to the opening line in Isaiah of the hymn of the suffering servant (Isaiah 42:1). Therefore, to be baptized into Christ is to be baptized into the suffering servant of God.

Thus, what Linda and those around Audrey observe each day are the apparent consequences of her baptism. For each day it appears that Audrey, like all victim souls, abandons herself completely to God for the sake of sinners.

While it is helpful to understand Audrey's apparent victimhood utilizing the many records and documentation, perhaps only through her mother can we more deeply grasp this mystery of suffering in Christ. For in God's choice of a child, especially one who cannot speak, we face an extraordinary number of baffling questions that must be answered by someone who has witnessed the events.

The following interview with Linda Santo directly relays her impression of what Audrey is experiencing.

Q: *Tell us about Audrey's suffering, especially during Easter.*

A: During Lent, Audrey is in so much pain. But beginning at three o'clock on Holy Thursday, there are times when she is just agitated. We would carefully, the nurse and I, hold her up above the bed. Audrey would then cry so much that you couldn't put her on the bed. That's how much pain she would be in. On Good Fridays she would be in intense pain till three o'clock. Then she suddenly would fall asleep. Audrey would go totally out at three o'clock, and her suffering would stop.

Q: *How long did Audrey sleep?*

A: Audrey would sleep sometimes until (Easter) Sunday morning. But she always sleeps on Holy Saturday, always. She's totally asleep. You can't wake her. You can't budge her. You can put her in and out of the bathtub and she still remains asleep. There are other Thursdays and Fridays during the year when lots of people come and ask for prayer, and again Audrey would do this. She would just begin to suffer. We would say to the people, "Audrey's really sick." So people couldn't see her for the next two days. Most of the time, the doctors would want to do something to make her better. But when you don't even know where the problem's coming from, you don't have a remedy. They would get frustrated.

Q: *What has happened as time has gone along? Since 1989, how much more has Audrey begun to suffer?*

A: The holes in her hands, the sufferings, these experiences, all became closer for some reason. Starting in 1989, these kinds of situations were ongoing. Sometimes Audrey would have clusters of suffering episodes. Perhaps say, this week and then for not two weeks. I don't know how to explain it. There was no rhyme or reason to it. It just depended, I guess, on what God was doing. As I said, she would suffer a lot during Lent. Often she would cry - copiously. This past Good Friday (1996), Audrey cried from the time Fr. Joyce opened the tabernacle. I mean, she cried and cried and cried. Not like a little tear here and there.

We're talking copious amounts of tears, to the point where Audrey's eyes are bloodshot, and her face is red. I mean, if you could imagine the most painful hurt that you would have and you would just cry over it, you know there are no words - you just cry and cry. This is what Audrey would do. She did that this year during Lent and during last year's Lent. There was also a lot of bleeding. Audrey bled from her trachea for a week and a half. She's had other experiences. When Audrey has bleeding experiences, she bleeds from almost every orifice of her body. It's not like I know how to explain it. There's blood from her nose, blood from her ears, blood from her mouth, blood from her trachea and from her hands and feet.

Q: *So, you're saying Audrey would bleed from her hands and her feet and her side, as well as her orifices?*

A: Yes, most especially her stomach.

Q: *You said that priests have said Audrey is suffering the Passion. Can you explain this?*

A: Well, Jesus was tortured, He was beaten, and when Jesus was beaten, this caused tremendous damage to the inside of Him. We tend to look at Christ's physical appearance, the wounds. And maybe it's best not to even know what went on inside of Christ, because the destruction was incredible. But this is how Audrey suffers. She suffers totally as Christ did.

Q: *Has Audrey had the "Crown of Thorns"?*

A: Yes. And it wasn't just a little "Crown of Thorns" - it was around her entire head. She had the "Crown of Thorns" on Holy Thursday in 1991 or 1992.

Q: *What did you see?*

A: A nurse called me over and said, "Look, look, look!"...So when I looked, I could see it was like the "Crown of Thorns". There were marks coming out of her head. They were purple. There were purple marks all around her head.

Q: *Were they bleeding?*

A: The marks were really outstanding. You could feel them if you rubbed your hand there. She had the marks for about six hours that day. Then Audrey had the "Crown of Thorns" again on Ascension Thursday of 1992, when my two older kids were in Medjugorje. And they (Linda's two oldest children) were actually making a "Crown of Thorns" for Audrey on Cross Mountain (Mt. Krizevac) at the time.

Q: *You said Audrey has suffered the Passion on repeated occasions. Can you explain this in detail?*

A: Audrey has suffered the Passion many, many times. Starting Thursday night, usually till Friday night. What happens is her hands excoriate. Then, she sometimes has the "Crown of Thorns". She bleeds from her nose, her mouth, her trachea, her ears. She can also have the phenomenon of weight and position, where she becomes too heavy to move and her heartbeat is rapid as if in ecstasy.

Q: *Describe this positional phenomenon of weight?*

A: Audrey will assume the position of the crucifixion.

Q: *Will she assume it in bed?*

A: Yes, Audrey bends backwards, she arches backwards. Then, she takes on what you would think is the face of Christ. You know, that look on the crucified face of Christ.

Q: *What else occurs?*

A: She'll stop breathing. On Good Friday, Audrey bled from her side on a number of occasions. She's even had blood in her mouth.

Q: *How many times have the wounds appeared on her hands?*

A: Well, it's not just Audrey's hands. She's had the "Crown of Thorns" twice, wounds in her side and her feet.

Q: *Could you describe the "side wound"?*

A: She bleeds from her side.

Q: *From her left side or right side?*

A: Her left side.

Q: *How big was the wound there?*

A: I'd have to look at the documentation to be exact, maybe a quarter of an inch.

Q: *Where do the whip marks appear?*
A: All over her body.
Q: *What do these marks look like?*
A: They are purple and red streaks.
Q: *When do they appear?*
A: They occur out of nowhere and then completely vanish. But when Audrey experiences the Passion, and I'd like to note this, because people have a view of just holes in the hands and the feet and the side. But that is not what Christ died of, Jesus died of asphyxiation. Everything inside His body failed -His kidneys, His liver, His heart, His lungs. When Audrey experiences the Passion, she experiences the entire Passion. By that I mean, the weight - you cannot move her. Then, she's in ecstasy for six to eight hours. Then she totally collapses at that point and is clinically dead. She expires.
Q: *Does her heart stop beating?*
A: Everything stops.
Q: *How many times has this occurred?*
A: Many, many, many, times. It's all documented. So when Audrey experiences things, her Passion may not just be a wound in her hand or wound in her side. That can happen and I don't mean to undermine or minimize other mystics. But Audrey is like a twelfth century mystic. She's in bed. She's an invalid. And she suffers the total Passion.
Q: *So, Audrey is kind of like a mystic of another time or era?*
A: Yes, she's what many mystics, to me, used to be like. For instance, people don't realize that Padre Pio would cough for eighteen hours. I mean we go "Ahem, Ahem" and we're agitated, you know what I mean? We may have a little cough and we're taking cough medicine. But Our Lord coughed, He coughed up blood. People aren't aware of the fact that while Christ was on the cross, they stuck a piece of wood up Him to hold Him there. He bled- He hemorrhaged. Audrey will do that also.
Q: Will she bleed rectally?

100

A: Yes. She'll bleed rectally. Today most people who see stigmatists concentrate on the hand wounds or the foot wounds or the side wounds. But the full Passion of Jesus is exactly that - the full Passion. Audrey's experiences are similar to those of Therese Neumann, Marthe Robin, you know, mystics that were in bed all the time.

Q: *How many times has Audrey experienced the full Passion?*

A: Over fifty times.

CHAPTER EIGHTEEN

SUFFERING IN FAITH

The sheer intensity of the events surrounding Audrey Santo over the three-year period of 1993-1996 is beyond full explanation. From her acute suffering to the dozens of weeping images around her, everything has been extremely powerful and ardent.

But if the images throughout the Santo home reflected Heaven's sadness, then it is necessary to ponder, before we go any further, the full meaning regarding this little child being apparently chosen by God to suffer.

For little Audrey Santo is, perhaps, a living sign to the world of what many believe remains the world's greatest mystery ever: *the Passion and Death of Jesus Christ for the salvation of the world.*

Specifically, what we are talking about here is the meaning of Christ's suffering, and for that matter, suffering as a whole? What purpose does it serve? Why do we suffer? And what does it mean to "suffer in Christ"?

But before we can understand what suffering as a victim in Christ is all about, we must understand the role of suffering for God's people. For Scripture slowly unravels this mystery, almost in the way a mother gradually introduces solid food to her child.

From a Scriptural standpoint, the Book of Job is generally viewed as an excellent starting point to examine the mystery of suffering. Scholars say that Job teaches a classical doctrine on the relationship of suffering to the human experience.

In the Prologue, Job is described as a faithful, wealthy man who was holy in the sight of God and his fellow man. But then, God acquiesces to the requests of Satan and submits Job to the test. Job loses everything, but nevertheless, he somehow maintains his trust in God. Consequently, through his suffering, he eventually triumphs. In the end, God restores Job as an example of the "suffering servant" who perseveres and triumphs in steady faith.

Throughout the Old Testament history of God's people, suffering was the road trod by every generation. From Adam and Eve's expulsion from the Garden of Eden to Moses' woes in the desert, from Jonah's helplessness in the belly of the whale to Daniel's terrifying confrontation in the lion's den, the Old Testament continually takes God's chosen ones down the lonely and bewildering road of suffering.

In every case, those who remain firm in faith until the end often discover the reason for their suffering, if not the restoration of their former glory.

Moreover, the Old Testament reveals how God tests His chosen ones so that they might prove their faith. Humility, the need for a pure heart, and God's joy in exalting His obedient ones are all lessons derived from suffering. Likewise, God exhorts His people to accept the importance of suffering because hope, consolation, patience and perseverance are derived from suffering, and this is the path which leads to wisdom.

While Old Testament stories regarding the sufferings of God's great servants abound, the prophets,too, spoke of the suffering of God's people. Whether because of sin or God's desire to teach, Scripture reveals a God who judges and wants to save all. Therefore, all suffering is oriented and directed to the fulfillment of God's plan of salvation for His people.

In the Book of Proverbs, suffering is shown to be related to the faith of the people. The faithful live rewarding lives, while the unfaithful become victims of their sin. In the Book of Daniel, Israel learns that God will punish the people for their sins by sending tribulation, for God is just. While in the Book of Sirach, God reminds His people that they are responsible for the sins which led to their suffering. **"For the wicked, these were created evil, and it is they who bring on destruction"** (Sir 40:10).[1]

Suffering, suffering and more suffering! God continues throughout the Old Testament to permit and justify His people's condition, constantly attempting to draw them closer to the great mystery not through fear, but through wisdom.

In the Book of Amos, God reveals that to be worthy of His love, people must expect that everything, including His justice, may cause suffering. Suffering may even come if one takes God's blessing too lightly.

In the Book of Micah, those who accept the Lord's blessing and then turn away should not be surprised at the consequences. **"When they cry to the Lord, He shall not answer them. Rather shall He hide His face from them at that time, because of the evil they have done" (Mi 3:4).[2]**

But it is with the writings of the prophet Isaiah where we begin to learn of one whose suffering is yet to come. He is the Christ, the suffering servant unlike any before.

Isaiah reveals the man of sorrow as the servant who is to be exalted through his suffering. For the mystery of this man is to be recognized. And through his humiliation, God's people will come to understand who he really is (Is 52:13-15).

Indeed, Isaiah foretells how God's people will also come to understand the true meaning of the Messiah's sufferings. For after believing that he is to be stricken for his own sins, they soon learn that he really suffers for them. Therefore, his suffering is necessary for their healing.

> **"Who would believe that we have**
> **heard?**
> **"To whom has the arm of the Lord**
> **been revealed?**
> **"He grew up like a sapling before him,**
> **like a shoot from the parched earth;**
> **"There was in him no stately bearing to make us**
> **look at him, nor appearance that would**
> **attract us to him.**
> **"He was spurned and avoided by men,**
> **a man of suffering, accustomed to infirmity,**
> **"One of those from whom men hide their faces,**

spurned and we held him in no esteem.
"Yet it was our infirmities that he bore,
   our sufferings that he endured.
"While we thought of him as stricken,
   as one smitten by God and afflicted,
"But he was pierced for our offenses,
   crushed for our sins;
"Upon him was the chastisement that
 makes us whole,
   by his stripes we were healed.
"We had all gone astray like sheep,
   each following his own way;
"But the Lord laid upon him
   the guilt of us all.
"Though he was harshly treated, he submitted
   and opened not his mouth;
"Like a lamb led to slaughter
   or a sheep before the shearers,
   he was silent and opened not his
   mouth.
"Oppressed and condemned, he was
   taken away,
   and who would have thought any
   more of his destiny?
"When he was cut off from the land of
   the living,
   and smitten for the sin of his people,
"A grave was assigned him among the
   wicked, and a burial place with evildoers,
"Though he had done no wrong
   nor spoken any falsehood.
"(But the Lord was pleased
   to crush him in infirmity.)
"If he gives his life as an offering for sin,
   he shall see his descendants in a long
   life, and the will of the Lord shall be
   accomplished through him.
"Because of his affliction,

he shall see the light in fullness of
days,
"Through his suffering, my servant shall
justify many,
and their guilt he shall bear.
"Therefore I will give him his portion
among the great,
and he shall divide the spoils with
the mighty,
"Because he surrendered himself to death
and was counted among the wicked;
"And he shall take away the sins of many,
and win pardon for their offenses."
(Is 53:1-12)[3]

With Isaiah's words comes the most profound concept of *"vicarious suffering"*, which the Messiah would undergo for his people. Most of all, God's people now understood that he would do it for their sins. Therefore, the Messiah would be an innocent victim, and God's people were now being profoundly called into the mystery of redemption. That is, they were discovering what it really meant and how this redemption would be fulfilled through one man's suffering.

Of course, this man was Jesus Christ, true man and true God. Isaiah clearly foretells that He is the one who emptied Himself by taking the form of a servant (Is 42:1) and by being born in the likeness of man. He then humbled Himself through obedience to the point of death upon the cross. Afterward, God exalted Him so **"that at Jesus's name every knee must bend in the heavens and on the earth, and under the earth, and every tongue proclaim to the glory of God the Father: JESUS CHRIST IS LORD!"** (Phil 2:10:11).[4]

Indeed, Jesus Christ is the ultimate suffering servant. He is the only Son of the Father who was sent as an offering for our sins (1 Jn 4:10). He is the victim soul who sacrificed Himself for our salvation (Ti 2:14) by His obedience to God the Father (Heb 5:8). Through His suffering, He was tested in order to help those who are tested (Heb 2:18).

Therefore, Christ's entire being was constantly subjected to sufferings, trials, and persecution. He submitted to this because of love, foremost being His love for His Father (Jn 14:31) followed by His love for all mankind (Jn 15:12-13).

Most significantly, Christ's sacrifice was worthy and absolutely perfect. Jesus was infinitely human and infinitely divine, thus fulfilling to the letter Isaiah's words about the perfect sacrifice.

But with Christ's "perfect sacrifice" came the secondary reality of what Scripture was teaching God's people concerning their own future sacrifices. For with Christ's sacrifice comes the invitation to offer ourselves for one another in order to be joined in Christ's body (1 Jn 4:11-16).

In other words, our attitude must be that of Christ (Phil 2:5). We must joyfully recognize in a new and most special way that the full concept and significance of vicarious suffering, as developed by Isaiah, can now be deeply understood. Because of Christ's Life, Passion, Death and Resurrection, suffering was now to be embraced and understood in the full wisdom that Scripture intended God's people to come to understand.

Likewise, the mystery of Co-Redemption is established and understood with our suffering in Christ, for as the Body of Christ, we are called to cooperate with Christ for the salvation of souls. Wrote St. Paul:

> **Even now I find joy in the suffering I endure for you. In my own flesh I fill up what is lacking in the sufferings of Christ for the sake of His body, the Church. I became a minister of this Church through the commission God gave me to preach among you His word in its fullness, that mystery hidden from ages and generations past but now revealed to His holy ones. God has willed to make known to them the glory beyond price which this mystery brings to the Gentiles - the mystery of Christ in you, your hope of glory. This is the Christ we proclaim while we admonish all men and teach them in the full measure of wisdom, hoping to make every man complete in Christ. For this I work and struggle, impelled by that energy of His which is so powerful a force within me** (Col 1:24-29).[5]

St. Paul struggled for this. His life and his words in Scripture confirm this reality. St. Paul was a victim soul, and he painstakingly and clearly defined this reality for us, so there would be no doubt about the profound message Christ was giving us through His own victimhood. St. Paul wrote:

> **The body is one and has many members, but all the members, many though they are, are one body; and so it is with Christ.**
>
> **If one member suffers, all the members suffer with it; if one member is honored, all the members share its joy** (1 Cor 12:12,26).[6]

With these words, we see how far God brings His people in their understanding of suffering. From the physical anguish of Adam and Eve as they departed the Garden ["**By the sweat of your face shall you get bread to eat**" (Gen 3:19)[7]] to the harsh words Moses received from the Lord announcing to His people their emotionally and psychologically painful exile ["**You will live in constant suspense and stand in dread both day and night, never sure of your existence. In the morning you will say. 'Would that it were evening!' and in the evening you will say 'Would that it were morning!' for the dread that your heart must feel and the sight that your eyes must see**" (Dt 28:66-67)[8]]; from Simeon's painful prophecy to Mary ["**and you yourself shall be pierced with a sword**" (Lk 2:35)[9]], to the anguish the crowd felt upon witnessing Christ's march to Calvary ["**a great crowd of people followed Him, including women who beat their breasts and lamented over Him**" (Luke 23:27)[10]], Scripture gradually and clearly leads us to become aware of the meaning and value of suffering. It then nurtures the ironic reality that all suffering can have a purpose. And by understanding God's words to His people through the ages, we learn that the ultimate purpose of suffering is to become Christ-like in accepting it.

But Scripture is also clear on how we come to this reality. It is a road that can only be traveled through faith. Even with all our human understanding and knowledge of the profound teachings regarding suffering, we will not bear fruit without strong roots. And these roots can only be planted through faith.

Likewise, with faith, God's people can then attempt to understand the next mystery of suffering: that of God's chosen victims who are singled out to share in Christ's cross in a special way.

For from St. Paul to St. Francis to perhaps little Audrey Santo, this mystery blinds our vision to all logic, in order to completely immerse our souls in the reality of what it means to be "crucified in Christ".

CHAPTER NINETEEN

THE LAST FRONTIER

How can a sweet, innocent little child be called upon as a victim in Christ? How can the harsh reality of this painful existence find any acceptance in our hearts and minds despite our belief in God's love and what our faith teaches?

Like all children, Audrey Santo harbors no hate, evil or sin for us to disdain. Instead, she radiates love and warmth, innocence and purity, compassion and tenderness. Most of all, in her helplessness, Audrey becomes a magnet drawing from all who see her every ounce of charity and hope which they so deeply desire to give to her.

Yet, the stark reality of the events surrounding Audrey's life demand our attention and lead us to ponder the only answer that holds merit, since explanations from the medical community have not come forth.

Admittedly, science cannot explain what happens to Audrey's body. It has not concluded that the red bleeding marks on her hands and feet are pathological in origin. It has not told us that her frequent welts and lacerations are being caused by something organic in nature. The experts have not explained why little Audrey weeps and weeps, sometimes tears of blood.

Today, medical science knows so very much about the human body; yet, it offers no answers when little Audrey Santo's heart races at 180 beats a minute for eight straight hours, when Audrey is frozen and unmovable and as heavy as lead, or when her head becomes covered with a circle of unnatural purple bumps. Indeed, despite medicine's advanced knowledge and the sophistication of its diagnostic tests, no plausible explanations have come forth as to why and what is happening to this little girl.

Most significantly, no medical answers have been forwarded as to why these physical experiences do not cause any true harm to this child. Rather, these bizarre physical manifestations of injury and disease unexplainably excuse themselves and disappear just as fast as they appear. Like the air Audrey breathes, they invisibly depart with their purpose apparently fulfilled. And this occurs right before the incredulous eyes of today's experts.

Dr. John Harding, M.D., Audrey's primary physician who visits her weekly, has stated that there just are no comfortable medical answers for what Audrey has, nor scientific explanations for her various conditions.[1] In other words, Audrey's physical manifestations cannot be explained. Therefore, only through faith may we conclude that Audrey's wounds and sufferings are understandable and serve a purpose. For in our faith, we are able to find answers to many "unexplainable" questions.

Since the beginning of time, answers steeped in faith easily slip into the picture when science is forced to relinquish its position of providing explanations. For all reality is not based upon knowledge and experience. Rather, as Scripture notes, wisdom begins with a fear of God, especially His words. And His words have endured and led generations to the truth about the meaning of life, especially when science falters and retreats.

But forwarding the belief that little Audrey's sufferings are mystical in nature may be akin to confronting the last of the great mysteries of our faith. For our computerized, highly technological world now has the ability to counter mystical phenomena by creating hybrid realities which challenge claims of the supernatural through almost perfect imitations of such phenomena.

Thus, statues can be effected to weep, computerized holographic images can project apparitions, and some faith healings can be proven to be psychological.

With these successes, a clever montage of explanations for all

111

supernatural events suddenly appears worthy enough to generate a sufficient amount of doubt in some people. And at that juncture, science then begins to lead an assault on God by forwarding the argument that its successes in debunking some alleged miracles are applicable to the whole realm of the supernatural.

And it doesn't stop there. This argument is then extended to the past, as contemporary intellectuals offer scientific, hypothetical situations intended to rebuke the supernatural legacy of great historical religious events. This has especially occurred with the events leading up to and after the resurrection of Christ. Therefore, today's intellectuals repeat what Cicero said thousands of years ago, *"What was incapable of happening never happened. And what was capable of happening is not a miracle. Consequently, there are no miracles."*

Yet in the events surrounding little Audrey Santo, we find great mysteries which do not shrink from science's tall stature. In fact, these mysteries have even challenged science to behold, examine and define what it sees, in order to offer an alternative explanation.

Carefully placed in the body of a child who cannot speak, some of the great mysteries of our faith have apparently held their ground and have accomplished what the great mysteries of the faith have done for centuries.

They have presented the truth once more. That truth explains how the greatest mystery of all — life itself — together with one of the greatest mysteries of faith — that suffering has a divine purpose — can converge to support the greatest truth ever given to the world: *Jesus Christ was and is God, and that Christ died on a cross and resurrected in order to redeem mankind of its sin!*

St. Paul, the apostle of suffering and victimhood, summarized this truth long ago in speaking of his own victimhood and its true meaning. He said, **"In my flesh I complete what is lacking in Christ's affliction for the sake of His body, that is, the Church"** (Col 1:24)[2]

But now, God has apparently again chosen *"His victim"* to continue what *"is lacking."* And for the faithful, the life of little Audrey Santo as a suffering servant, like the life of St. Paul, leads us beyond the reality of this apparent truth toward even more questions we can't help but ask.

112

Questions such as, why are certain souls "chosen"? What does Christ wish from them by having them suffer like He did? What is the total meaning of being uniquely chosen as a victim in Christ's love? And who are these souls that God calls to imitate His very self?

To begin with, all victim souls share three things in common. First, they are chosen by God ["**You did not choose me, but I chose you...**" (Jn 15:16)]. Secondly, through their prayers and intense devotions to the "Passion of Our Lord", their sufferings are meant to be offered up to God in union with His will. Finally, the great mystics tell us that this mystery always involves love. For love, it is said, is the mystical nurse who helps souls destined for heaven. Likewise, purity is a necessity. Together, love and purity permit a victim soul to actively imitate Christ in self-sacrifice, which is the supreme form of all love.

In Scripture, Christ said, "**No one has greater love than this, to lay down one's life for one's friends.**"(Jn 15:13) Therefore, victim souls raise up love to the degree that it assumes a form similar to Christ's. Victim souls sacrifice themselves for Christ's sake because they see Christ in souls, and therefore, whoever saves a soul, is saving Christ in that soul. Thus, they also adore, pray and expiate while in the world, always living with one thought in mind, that of consoling Christ by redeeming souls.

Scripture reveals that souls are redeemed by sacrifice. And in order to do this, victim souls carry two crosses. The first is the cross of Christ, which they desire to carry. The second is the cross of their brethren. As victim souls are permitted to see the future, often seeing an ocean of sorrows, they then perceive the loss of God forever for those souls whose sins go without reparation. Therefore, victim souls expiate for love of their brothers and sisters. They love in atonement to a heroic degree, while remaining in constant prayer.

Moreover, while victim souls suffer a tortured existence, they are further anguished by the reality of the spiritual miseries borne by souls of their fellow creatures. They see the wreckage of sin which erases the gifts of God in a soul. And so they take on the sufferings of the flesh, the heart, the mind, and the spirit in order to bring the graces necessary to rescue a soul for Heaven from the grasp of the Evil One.

Most of all, it is essential to understand how victim souls come to totally understand and embrace God's will in their lives. And the key to understanding this is their total abandonment to Christ. For whether overwhelmed by pain or plagued by attacks from Satan, their helplessness is exactly what God desires in order to lead them to fulfill their mission.

Over time, numerous revelations have defined the specific ways God's chosen ones sacrifice for sinners. Primarily though, it is through **reparation, expiation** and **atonement**.

Through *reparation*, a victim soul, by means of prayer and sacrifice, attempts to appease divine justice by appealing to God's mercy to forgive the sinner. In order to obtain this mercy, the victim soul shares in the agony of the cross. Therefore, the victim offers acts of reparation for the infidelities of sinners.

Expiation involves the victim soul's acceptance of others' punishments in order to appease divine justice. The victim soul takes on these sufferings and unites them with the cross of Christ. This is often a total immersion in Christ's Passion. When victim souls expiate for sin, they are acting on Christ's behalf as co-redeemers. Often the visible or invisible stigmata is the reward given to the victim soul.

Finally, *atonement* is more or less the call to vicarious suffering. That is, a victim soul literally suffers on behalf of another. It involves personal sacrifice and denial, and it is the supreme act of charity.

Most of all, it is important to understand that a victim soul's identification with Jesus' suffering is an identification with Jesus' loving, and nothing else. As Father Emmanuel explains,

"It is not mere animal pain that saves. It is love that saves, because God is love and only God can overcome evil and death in all of their manifestations. It is therefore of critical importance to recognize that the term "victim soul" does not mean that God is a victimizer. God chooses souls to love, like He loves. That is, to love like Christ loves. But, in a world drenched in evil, where mercilessness is rewarded and honored, the choices of "Christ like love" will almost inevitably make one a victim of evil. It is Satan not God, who victimizes. However, since "Christ like love" is the power of God, the apparent victim will in the end be the victor. The Lamb who was slain, the suffering servant, will conquer. The 'Good Friday' of the victim soul, the suffering servant, must give way to 'Easter Sunday' because God, who is Father, who is love, is almighty.

Although anyone may be "chosen" as a victim soul, onlookers must realize that these chosen ones are extraordinary. They are pure and holy souls, who although unworthy of their vocation, are the very elite of God's flock.

But while the Church has recorded a rich legacy of stigmatists, little Audrey Santo's life presents a challenge to even the most knowledgeable theologian. For apparently at the age of four, Audrey was chosen to be Christ's victim. Thus, victimhood as a child may be truly the *last frontier.*

Josyp Terelya, the Ukrainian Catholic visionary who spent twenty years in a Soviet gulag, spoke of the uniqueness of Audrey's life and mission. In the Mercy Foundation's documentary, *Audrey's Life*, Terelya said:

> I see her as a very special symbol. This child represents God's providence. She is a picture of the condition of the Church at this end part of the twentieth century. This is a warning to all the world not to remain sleeping and not to remain silent when we are confronted with evil and sin. We must love one another and love our God.[3]

Indeed, this mystery certainly discloses much about who little Audrey Santo must be and what her relationship with God must involve. But more than that, as Josyp Terelya noted, this mystery makes known the apparent state of a world where Heaven now moves in such a unique and mysterious way as to seemingly need expiation from a child, especially a child who is innocent and silent.

For Fr. Emmanuel, it is especially Audrey's silence that he believes draws her even closer to imitating the Lord. For in Scripture, beginning in the Book of Isaiah until Christ's crucifixion, the Lord's silence to a great degree constituted His mission as the suffering servant who fulfills the Will of God. Explained Fr. Emmanuel:

In the Suffering Servant, beginning with Isaiah 42:1, we are dealing with someone who is crushed by suffering but does not raise his voice in objection. In this process, because of the willing acceptance of the suffering, God is able to bring salvation to the world. Identification of Jesus as the Suffering Servant is the original identification of Jesus in the New Testament. We see it at the beginning of Jesus public ministry when he is baptized in the River Jordan. Arising out of the waters, Jesus hears the voice of God say **"This is my beloved Son in whom I am well pleased."** This is a direct reference to the hymn of the Suffering Servant in the Old Testament.

Audrey, and even her family, in this context are getting hit by incredible suffering. Yet, everyone is responding in a Christ-like way, in silent trustful love of God and each other.

What's taking place here is another moment in the mystery of God, bringing unimagined good out of incredible suffering.

Silence here is such a mystery. The Suffering Servant of the Old Testament was silent. Jesus was the silent, suffering servant in front of Pilate. And if we think about it, there have been so many more silent sufferers: The Holy Innocents, children in war, children in abortion, even the children in the sweatshops. Most people who suffer under evil are silent. But the silence doesn't mean God isn't active and present. Rather, He is working for the salvation of the world through them.

What it means is that these are the little ones, "anawim" in Biblical Hebrew, meaning "the little nobodies", who are forever crushed by the powers of the world, but who the Bible and Jesus tell us are God's chosen friends. Christ is with "the little nobodies" of the world and therefore when we help the helpless, love the unlovable or use our talents and treasure to care for the "least" we are actually encountering Christ. How do we know this? We know it because Christ explicitly said so in His famous last judgement sermon: **"What ever**

116

you do to the least you do to me" and **"What ever you neglect to do for the least you neglect to do for me."** (Mt 25:40,45)

Pain and suffering render people mute, but Jesus is on their side, indeed, He is deeply united with them. We must become the ones who become the voice for the voiceless. Linda and her family, through this great suffering, have become the voice for Audrey, who has become a voice for others? But who is to become the voice of all the hundreds of millions of other "Audreys" who are suffering in silence, in the wombs, the wars, in the sweatshops?

As an expression of the spiritual dimension, Audrey may be remembered in history, her suffering and silence becoming an example that can magnify on a grand scale the silent suffering of all other "Audreys". And Linda and her family may also be remembered in history as given a prophetic witness to the Gospel because of how they have responded with a total gift of their lives to the silent suffering of Audrey, "a little nobody by the worlds standards." There response is prophetic because it is the antithesis of how the world responds to all the "Audreys", because it is how God wants all people, in all places, and at all times to respond to the suffering "nobodies".

Fr. Emmanuel's words echo Heaven's wisdom, for according to the Virgin Mary's messages to the world over the last two hundred years, the world has become a dark, callous and dangerous place, a place where hate rules and "crucified innocence" is widespread. Ever since the apparitions of the Virgin Mary to St. Catherine Labouré at Rue du Bac, Paris in 1830, Heaven has been trying to warn us of our disintegrating state and how the world needs to convert before it's too late. This was also the message the Virgin brought at La Salette, Lourdes and Fatima.

Likewise, no sooner had Mary begun to appear at Medjugorje in June of 1981, than she immediately told the six children there, **"It is necessary for the world to be saved while there is still time"** (11/12/81).[4] And the Virgin added, "...**the only thing that I**

want to tell you is to be converted. Make that known to all my children as quickly as possible" (6/24/83).[5]

Indeed, ever since the apparitions of the Virgin Mary to St. Catherine Labouré, theologians have said that a divine plan has been unfolding through Mary's revelations. It is a plan that both the Queen of Heaven in her apparitions and Pope John Paul II in his writings (see *Crossing the Threshold of Hope*, page 221) have declared is *"close to fulfillment."*

Most significantly, it must be especially noted that throughout the centuries, God has consistently brought this plan to the world through children. For from La Salette to Lourdes, and from Fatima to Medjugorje, God has repeatedly singled out His youngest servants to carry His loving message of salvation to His people.

In the next several chapters, let us take a look at the unfolding of this plan over the centuries. Let us see how it so often involved children. And then let us contemplate how perhaps the life and mission of little Audrey Santo, as those closest to her believe, may be connected to it all.

PART IV

DEAR LITTLE FRIENDS

CHAPTER TWENTY

CHOSEN CHILDREN

When experienced doctors of theology contemplate how and why God sometimes chooses children to fulfill His plan, they often struggle to accept the logic and beauty of it. It baffles them, but simultaneously encourages speculative thought. But once they distance themselves from their human preconceptions of the limitations of a child, they are then able to marvel at how infinitely perfect children can be in the work of the Spirit.

As theologians know that God cannot err in His methodology, their conclusions supporting His wisdom in these matters are painstakingly tedious. But instead of complicated, the issue can perhaps be reduced to something quite simple. For a mere glance at the paintings of the masters, so abundantly filled with cherubs, is abundant proof of how much God cherishes children.

Indeed, the great frescoes of the Vatican say it all. Most notably, these works of the human hand are said to be quite accurate in their portrayal of the celestial playground above. For mystics and visionaries over the centuries have reported visions that confirm such a make-up of Heaven's court. Even Ivan Dragicevic, the visionary whom Audrey accompanied during attendance at her two apparitions in Medjugorje, has humorously explained that the angels who occasionally escort the Virgin Mary in her apparitions look almost like babies with wings.

And why not? If human beings cannot help to love and cherish children more than anything else on earth, isn't it natural that God, their Creator, should feel the same?

The beauty, warmth, purity, innocence and love of children are without comparison in the human experience. Children are God's most exquisite flowers, planted everywhere to blossom and grow in purity, and they steadily and consistently remind us what life is all about.

One look at a child, any child, is often enough to make a soul put his feet back on the ground. For little ones radiate and attract love in its most uncompromising state, thus freeing adults to discard the troubles and worries of everyday life. Then, after liberating us, they invite us to be young once again — young, pure, innocent and most of all, God-like in our own love and actions.

But if childhood is the most God-like period of the human condition, then the question of why God chooses children in the work of salvation is simple and evident. The purity of their souls, minds and hearts makes them perfect receivers and instruments for God's inspiration and direction.

Over the centuries there has been a significant number of chosen children, such as St. Philomena, St. Tarcisius, St. Agnes and St. Maria Goretti. But although Scripture and Church history are certainly filled with accounts of God accomplishing His will through little ones, it is especially intriguing to examine those stories that go beyond the ordinary.

These are the accounts of children who were "chosen" for important, historical missions. These are children who received apparitions and visions. These are children who heard God's voice and played with His angels, children that understood the ways of the Spirit and delighted in God's love for them. Most importantly, these children were obedient and, if called to, even suffered for the Lord.

Theologians have every right to scrutinize the essence of these accounts, for these stories are fascinating in their uniqueness and present spiritual expeditions into uncharted territory. Most of all, they take the faithful to higher levels of wonder and awe in the Lord. Indeed, the accounts of children participating in the mystical world are quite compelling and intriguing.

Who are these "chosen" children? There have been, and continue to be, many chosen little ones, long before Audrey Santo, as in the following story of a chosen child:

> A few days before She reached the age of three years, She was favored with an abstract vision of the Divinity, in which it was made known to Her that the time of Her departure for the temple ordained by God had arrived, and that there She was to live dedicated and consecrated to His service. Her most pure soul was filled with new joy and gratitude at this prospect and speaking with the Lord, She gave Him thanks saying: "Most high God of Abraham, Isaac and Jacob, my eternal and highest Good, since I cannot praise Thee worthily, let it be done in the name of this humble slave by the angelic spirits; since Thou immense Lord, who hast need of none, dost look upon this lowly wormlet of the earth in Thy unbounded mercy. Whence this great benefit to me, that Thou shouldst receive me into Thy house and service, since I do not even merit the most abject spot of the earth for my place of habitation? But as Thou art urged thereto by Thy own greatness, I beseech Thee to inspire the hearts of my parents to fulfill Thy holy will."[1]

Visions at the age of three? A dialogue with God? According to the Venerable Mary of Agreda, this child's supernatural experiences actually began as an infant. But this should not surprise us, for Mary of Agreda is revealing the life of the Virgin Mary in this account. And Mary was certainly worthy of such gifts as she was pure and without sin from the moment of conception.

Interestingly, the history of the Christian faith reveals a rich legacy of children who were touched in a special way by the hand of God. These stories go back to the beginning of the Church and are found in almost every century. Indeed, Church history has acknowledged and honored these children as "chosen".

One such soul was St. Catherine of Alexandria, a third-century virgin and martyr, who reported that when she was a child, a vision of Our Lady and the Holy Child instigated her conversion. She later died for the faith. In the fifth century, St. Martin of Tours reportedly received a vision as a young boy of Jesus Christ surrounded by angels. Like so many holy people in Scripture, he was led by dreams, and he eventually become the Patron Saint of France. At the age of six, St. Catherine of Siena (1347-1380) reported a vision of Christ seated in glory with the Apostles, Peter, Paul and John. She would later become a Doctor of the Church.

In the fifteenth century, St. Joan of Arc said that at the age of fourteen, she heard heavenly voices. She claimed they carried messages from God. The French martyr also reported visions of St. Michael, St. Catherine of Alexandria and St. Margaret, the three saints whose images stood in front of the church in her village of Domrémy.

Four hundred years later, St. John Bosco became another chosen child. He was called to a special mission in the service of the Lord. Born in 1815, he was especially renowned for his dreams, visions and prophecies. In 1858, Pope Pius IX ordered John Bosco to write down all his dreams for posterity. This required St. John Bosco to detail in his memoirs a dream he received at the age of nine that he never forgot. Wrote St. John Bosco:

> When I was about nine years old, I had a dream that left a profound impression on me for the rest of my life. I dreamed that I was near my home, in a very large playing field where a crowd of children was having fun. Some were laughing, others were playing, and not a few were cursing. I was so shocked at their language that I jumped into their midst, swinging wildly and shouting at them to stop. At that moment, a man appeared, nobly attired with a manly and imposing bearing. He was clad with a white flowing mantle, and his face radiated such light that I could not look directly at him. He called me by name and told me to place myself as leader over those boys, adding the words, "You will have to win these friends of yours not with blows, but with gentleness and kindness. So begin right now to show them that sin is ugly and virtue beautiful."
>
> Confused and afraid, I replied that I was only a boy and unable to talk to these youngsters about religion. At that moment the fighting, shouting and cursing stopped, and the crowd of boys gathered about the man who was

now talking. Almost unconsciously, I asked: "But how can you order me to do something that looks so impossible?"

What seems so impossible you must achieve by being obedient and by acquiring knowledge."

But where, how?"

"I will give you a teacher, under whose guidance you will learn and without whose help all knowledge becomes foolishness."

"But who are you?"

"I am the Son of Her whom your mother has taught you to greet three times a day."

"My mother told me not to talk to people I don't know unless she gives me permission. So, please tell me your name."

At that moment I saw beside Him a Lady of majestic appearance, wearing a beautiful mantle glowing as if bedecked with stars. She saw my confusion mount, so she beckoned me to her. Taking my hand with great kindness, she said: "Look!"

I did so. All the children had vanished. In their place I saw many animals: goats, dogs, cats, bears and a variety of others.

"This is your field, this is where you must work," the Lady told me. "Make yourself humble, steadfast, and strong. And what you will see happen to these animals you will have to do for my children."

I looked again; the wild animals had turned into as many lambs, gently gamboling lambs, bleating a welcome for that Man and Lady.

At this point of my dream I started to cry and begged the Lady to explain what it all meant because I was so confused. She then placed her hand on my head and said: "In due time everything will be clear to you."

After she had spoken these words, some noise awoke me; everything had vanished.[2]

The next day, St. John Bosco's mother, after hearing of the dream, said, "Who knows if someday my son may not become a priest."³

Today, also, with the era of the modern-day apparitions of the Virgin Mary, we find God repeatedly singling out children to be the instruments of a divine plan of mercy.

It is a plan that seems to be mounting to a climax, a climax which was revealed to St. John Bosco in what has become his most famous dream ever: The Two Columns. In this dream full of interesting imagery, St. John Bosco foretold that after an extended period of turmoil, the Church would triumph with the aid of a strong Pope, the Blessed Virgin Mary and the Eucharist.

Theologians certainly agree that this era began in 1830 in Paris with the Virgin Mary's apparitions to St. Catherine Labouré, a sister in the Daughters of Charity. St. Catherine was twenty-four at the time of the apparitions, but Heaven had introduced itself to her long before the extraordinary manifestations began.

St. Catherine's mother died when she was just nine, causing her to declare that the Virgin Mary was now her mother. This declaration led to a second affirmation. The child earnestly repeated that she would one day "see" the Mother of God.

Shortly thereafter, St. Catherine received her First Holy Communion. At the age of eleven, her whole life radically changed. Her sister, Tonine, recalled that Catherine became "entirely mystical." Catherine especially detailed a dream in which she was told by a priest, *"God has plans for you, do not forget it."*⁴

But most importantly, St. Catherine was to be the heralding voice of the coming of a great battle between the forces of light and the forces of darkness. It would be a battle, visionaries foretold, that would certainly be decisive in many ways.

According to Marian experts, Mary's apparitions to St. Catherine Labouré on July 18, 1830, at Rue du Bac, Paris were monumental. For the prophecies which Mary gave her declared that sweeping changes were about to come into the entire world. These changes would alter the course of human history.

"The times are evil," Mary told St. Catherine. **"The whole world will be upset by miseries of every kind."** ⁵

Mary then told St. Catherine that by the time everything prophesied had climaxed, no one would be left untouched. **"My child,** the whole world will be in sadness."[6]

No sooner had Catherine's experiences of that day ended, than events in Paris began to develop. On July 27, 1830, a revolution erupted in fury. In just days, numbers of dead lay in the streets, as constitutional monarchists, middle-class shopkeepers, extreme radicals, and a Parisian mob united against King Charles X. The "three glorious days" of the July revolution followed, as King Charles was overthrown and exiled to England.

"For throne and altar" had been the motto of King Charles, and the Church had prospered under him. But now, his godless enemies ran wild, desecrating churches, overturning statues and trampling crosses under foot, just as Mary had foretold to St. Catherine. These events were indeed tragic and unprecedented, but there was more to come.

Saturday, November 27, 1830, began as just a routine day for Catherine Labouré. But soon, it became one of the greatest days in Church history, as Mary again appeared to Catherine that evening. Two remarkable visions would lead to the striking of the Miraculous Medal.

With the sound of wind rushing through the room, the Queen of Heaven appeared. This time she was standing upon a globe in *"all her perfect beauty,"* recalled Catherine.

Mary's eyes were raised heavenward, and she held in her hands a golden ball which she seemed to offer to God. Then her hands became resplendent with rings set with precious stones that glittered and flashed in a brilliant cascade of lights.

"**The ball which you see,**" Mary told Catherine, "**represents the world, especially France, and each person in particular. The rays symbolize the graces I shed upon those who ask for them. The gems from which rays do not fall are the graces for which souls forget to ask.**" [7]

The golden ball then disappeared from Mary's hands. Suddenly, Mary's arms swept open in a wide gesture of motherly compassion, as her fingers projected streams of white light upon the globe at her feet. An oval frame formed around Mary, and written within it in letters of gold were the words:

"**O Mary, conceived without sin, pray for us who have recourse to thee.**"

The significance of the three visions experienced by St.

Catherine that day are detailed in numerous books. The Miraculous Medal is quite often the focal point of these chronicles.

But the second and third visions in particular revealed a special message without equal, just as did the Virgin's words to her on July 18, 1830. Indeed, Mary's words and visions foretelling global events to St. Catherine were unprecedented.

Moreover, never before had Mary come in such a remarkable fashion. Prior to her visitations to St. Catherine, the Virgin's apparitions were scattered over the centuries, and her heavenly admonitions were most often local and, at the very most, regional. And while other great mystics of this particular era, such as the Venerable Catherine Emmerich, disclosed their own visions and prophecies which also had world-wide implications, these types of revelations were never given in such a definitive and conclusive manner as occurred with St. Catherine Labouré at Rue du Bac.

Indeed, St. Catherine was given a world-wide mission unlike any before. Likewise, the overall importance of what transpired at Rue du Bac was also a singular grace in many ways. And all this confirmed the supreme importance of the Rue du Bac apparitions in the unfolding of a plan designed to "*save the world*," as Mary would later declare at Fatima and Medjugorje.

Fr. Joseph Dirvin, C.M., in his book, *St. Catherine Labouré of the Miraculous Medal,* noted the incredible significance of Heaven choosing Catherine as a child and then nurturing and preparing her for her important mission. He wrote, "In other famous appearances to chosen souls, Our Lady has burst suddenly upon their sight, as it were, from out of nowhere. Here, her coming was a calm logical climax to years of intimacy." [8]

St. Catherine died in 1876; when her body was exhumed in 1933, it was found incorrupt. This further implied an almost sinless and perfect life in the eyes of God.

Thus, at Rue du Bac, God began the "Age of Mary" with a chosen individual who was but a child when He first began to work in her.

But with the revelations to Saint Catherine, a wave of human and spiritual events soon revealed the nature, as well as the reality, of Mary's words at Rue du Bac in 1830. Indeed, the times were evil, and it wasn't an evil that had appeared from nowhere.

CHAPTER TWENTY-ONE

HIDDEN FROM THE WISE

While Satan's presence and influence have been in existence since the beginning, according to many Christian writers, a heightened era of demonic activity arose in the late Middle Ages. This trend toward evil became especially apparent in the writings and teachings of the philosophers of the age, many of whom began to challenge anything that was not confirmed by the senses. A particular target of their attacks was religious teaching.

As far back as the sixteenth century, French philosopher René Descartes (1596-1650) believed and taught that every concept should be questioned or doubted until reason proved its validity. This philosophy of emphasizing human reason to determine truth became known as Rationalism. After this, philosophers stressed the exaltation of reason and proposed philosophies that had one thing in common: faith of any sort, including Christianity, could not be a component of the philosophy. Those who maintained any droplet of faith were disparagingly referred to as "unenlightened". These philosophies quickly blended into the politics of the era, as philosophers such as Kant, Leibnitz and England's Lord Herbert of Cherbury pushed for a new religion of "unity".

The next step was the appearance of a wave of philosophers who were known to be anti-God, especially anti-Christian and anti-Catholic. Voltaire (1694-1778) mocked Christianity and was one of the leaders of the movement toward new societies of free thinkers, called Freemasons. Other philosophies, such as those espoused by French philosopher Pierre Bayle, mocked the Bible and insisted it was no different than any other book. The German philosopher, Nietzsche, was strongly anti-God and declared that a new "creator" was needed.

Not surprisingly, by the nineteenth century some of these philosophies had been integrated into the social mentality of the times, where their evil roots became even more discernible.

Not long after Rue du Bac, two more French children were again singled out to become tools of the Almighty in order to combat and define the rising tide of evil in the world. On September 19, 1846, Maximin Giraud and Melanie Calvat were graced by an apparition of the Virgin Mary near the mountainous village of La Salette, France.

Maximin was eleven years old and Melanie was fourteen years old at the time. The apparitions, like those at Rue du Bac to St. Catherine, were eventually approved by the Church. And just as at Rue du Bac, Mary continued to explain that vast, sweeping changes were approaching. "**The whole world will be upse**t," Mary told Melanie, "**by miseries of every kind.**"

But Melanie Calvat, to whom the Virgin detailed a long, apocalyptic, secret message during the apparition, had been experiencing supernatural graces long before the apparitions at La Salette.

Melanie was an unloved, abused child who early in life took refuge in conversation with her "little brother", who was actually Jesus appearing to her as a little boy.

In a fit of rage, Melanie's mother threw her daughter out of the home at the tender age of three, and told her to live in the woods behind their house. After running down a path, the child found a log and cried herself to sleep. Melanie said she then received a strange dream of a little boy her age wearing a white wreath on his head, the kind of wreath the children wore for First Holy Communion. The little boy in her dream comforted her and told her to call him "brother".

"I am your good brother," he told Melanie. "I will take care of you. We have a mother."[1]

"A mother! A mother!" cried Melanie, weeping in her dream. "Where is she, brother, so that I may run quickly and find her?"[2]

130

"Someday, I will take you to see Our Mother," said the boy. After that, the little boy told Melanie about God and the life and death of Jesus Christ.[3]

Melanie listened attentively and replied, "I too want to suffer, like the good Jesus. Oh, I wouldn't dare enter heaven if I didn't suffer like the good Lord."[4]

"Where would you like to go?" the little boy asked her.

"To Calvary," Melanie answered.[5]

The little boy in her dream then took her on path that led up a steep hill. The sky darkened and it began to rain crosses, little and big crosses. The crosses almost buried Melanie, but she insisted on staying with the boy, even though she was ridiculed and taunted by a crowd of people that appeared.

Melanie awoke to find that she was under an oak tree, and the sun was rising. Suddenly, she heard a voice cry out, "Sister!" She turned, and there to her delight, was the same little boy, still wearing the crown of white roses. The boy gave her something to drink and asked her, "What favor would you like?"

"If it is the wish of Almighty God, I should like to serve Him in the way of the cross."[6]

The little boy then touched his hands on Melanie's head, hands, feet and heart. At this, as a little child, Melanie Calvat was given the stigmata.

And with the stigmata, Melanie immediately felt pain in those parts of her body. Later in life, particularly on Fridays and during Lent, sores would form, and blood would exude from her wounds. Like other stigmatists, Melanie's wounds would often heal and vanish without scarring.

After several days, Melanie's father came and found her. Her story mystified him, but throughout her life she never doubted that this friend had been the Christ Child.

No child picked by God is better known than St. Bernadette Soubirous. Honest, intelligent, and straightforward, Bernadette has become the model child visionary. At fourteen, she received eighteen apparitions of the Virgin Mary beginning in February of 1858. Included in these apparitions was one of the most famous moments in the history of visions, when the Virgin declared to Bernadette, "**I am the Immaculate Conception.**"

The fact that this monumental disclosure was made to a child is a significant point in understanding the ways of God. For since the sealing of Divine Revelation with the death of the Apostles, no other private revelation has so marked the unfolding of the mysteries of our faith.

The Church had acknowledged the truth of the Immaculate Conception on December 8, 1854. But with her apparition to Bernadette in Lourdes, Mary herself was now signing the Bull. And the Virgin was summing it up in a more definitive manner than any churchman had ever dreamed of until then. But shortly afterward, Heaven chose yet more children to use in a very special way to forward its plan.

About two hundred miles to the west of Paris lies the village of Pontmain. One night in 1871, the Virgin Mary again appeared to four children: Eugene Barbadette, age twelve, Joseph Barbadette, age ten, Francoise Richer, age eleven, and Jeanne Marie LeBosse, who was nine. There was perhaps a fifth visionary, whom history leaves unnamed: a two year-old child held in the arms of her mother on that fateful night, clapped her hands in excitement and then stretched out her arms toward the area of the sky where Mary was reported to be.

At that time, France was at war with Prussia, and the invaders were nearly at the entrance of Pontmain. Mary asked the children for prayer and promised that God would hear their petitions. This was exactly what occurred, as the war ended days later.

In the nineteenth century, France had received four apparitions (Rue du Bac, La Salette, Lourdes, and Pontmain), all of which were approved by the Church, yet the country continued to spiritually collapse along with the rest of Europe. Mary's words to St. Catherine Labouré at Ru du Bac were slowly coming true, as the entire world seemed to be surrendering to evil.

But God continued to send help. Once again, this help came to France.

St. Therese of Lisieux may very well be the saint most people of our times pray to. Even Pope Pius X declared as much. But we often fail to remember or even realize that St. Therese was but a child when she was called.

Marie Francoise Therese Martin was born in 1873, and at the age of thirteen, she experienced her complete conversion and began to "long to work for the conversion of sinners with a passion." Indeed, Therese confesses in her autobiography, *The Story of a Soul,* that by fourteen she "understood the secrets of perfection." It was an understanding, the Little Flower wrote, that only a verse of Scripture could explain. Wrote St. Therese:

> When a gardener takes trouble over fruit he wants to ripen early, it isn't because he wants to leave them hanging on the tree, but because he wants them to appear on a richly appointed table. It was the same reason that made Jesus shower His favors on His little flower. During His days on earth He exclaimed in a transport of joy: **"I give Thee praise that Thou hast hidden all this from the wise and prudent, and revealed it to little children."** As Jesus wished to make His mercy evident through me as I was small and weak, He stooped down to me and secretly taught me the secrets of His love.[7]

What is equally true (though not implied by St. Therese) is that the secrets of God's love are children. Scripture voices Christ's words loudly and clearly concerning Heaven's view of children, not just because of their helplessness, but because of their godliness. Clearly, St. Therese was another chosen "child" for the times.

St. Therese's childhood call was just the beginning of many similar calls in the nineteenth and twentieth centuries. Soon afterward, several others were chosen. These young, innocent souls were taken from the world before they ever knew it and immediately sent into battle for the Lord. Meanwhile, an increasing number of prophets, mystics and visionaries continued to declare the approach of an epic period in the history of mankind.

St. Maximilian Kolbe was born on January 8, 1889, and at the age of ten, he received an apparition of the Virgin Mary. The Madonna presented two crowns to the young boy, a white one and a red one. Mary told Maximilian that the white crown meant he would remain pure, and the red one meant he would die a martyr. The Virgin wanted to know which one he would choose.

Maximilian Kolbe chose both. Afterward, his work as a saintly priest and publisher-founder of the periodical, *Knight of the Immaculate,* eventually landed him in Auschwitz, where Maximilian Kolbe gave his life for a fellow prisoner.

At the turn of the century, another young man was chosen by God for the times. This saintly soul joined the Capuchin order and was ordained in 1910. He would go on to become possibly the most famous stigmatist of our time.

But by the age of five, Francisco Gorgione had already received an apparition of the Sacred Heart of Jesus, and he had offered himself as Christ's victim.

Indeed, "Padre Pio", as the world would come to know him, is said to have been a holy boy who liked to be by himself. Listening to heavenly voices and spending time absorbed in prayer, little Francisco lived a mystical childhood that led to a life of heroic service on behalf of the Lord.

Little Nelly of Holy God lived around the same time as Padre Pio. She has come to be known as "The Violet of the Holy Eucharist". Little Nelly was born in the village of Portlow, County Waterford, Ireland. Although she died before the age of five, her short life is a heroic testimony to the True Presence of Christ in the Eucharist.

Orphaned at two years of age because of her mother's death and the resulting separation of family, Little Nelly came to live with the Good Shepherd Sisters at Sunday's Well, Cork. There, Nelly began to experience a series of physical ailments that eventually led to her death. But during her brief life of suffering, she was quickly recognized as a chosen soul, for she received great graces that drew her to love the Lord, especially in the Blessed Sacrament.

At three years of age, Little Nelly often reported speaking to "Holy God". She also reported an unexplainable urge to receive the Eucharist, which first occurred when she was four by the local bishop's decree.

Prophetic statements, ecstasies, and surviving on only Holy Communion characterized her brief life. Little Nelly died on February 2, 1908. And not long afterward, Pope Pius X began a review of her life. To this day, she is still known for her powerful intercessions, as people throughout the world turn to the saintly child to receive special help from "Holy God".

But it was during World War I that God called to His service the best known child visionaries of all time.

In 1917, three shepherd children in the village of Fatima, Portugal reported seven apparitions of the Virgin Mary from May 13th through October 13th of that year. The three children were Lucia Santos, age ten, Jacinta Marto, age nine, and her brother, Francisco Marto, age seven.

Curiously, Lucia's memoirs reveal that even before the apparitions of Mary, Heaven had already graced her in a special way. When she was six, right after going to her first confession, Lucia knelt before a statue of the Virgin Mary in church to offer a special prayer. Suddenly, to her amazement, a miracle occurred. Wrote John Haffert, in his book, *Her Own Words,* "The statue smiled at her and with a loving look and gesture, reassured her that her prayer had been heard."[8]

Likewise, Haffert reported that in her memoirs, Lucia recalled having witnessed an angel in 1915 at the age of eight. She wrote, "We saw a figure poised in the air above the trees. It looked like 'a statue made of snow' or a 'person wrapped in a sheet'."[9] Then in 1916, the year before the apparitions of Mary, the three children received several more apparitions of an angel.

But it is in the Fatima revelations themselves, that once again we are presented with the significance of God choosing children. At Fatima, Mary left secrets dealing with the future of the world. The most serious of these secrets dealt with the end of World War I, the prediction of World War II, the rise of Communism in Russia and the coming of the "Triumph of the Immaculate Heart of Mary". This "Triumph", Mary told Lucia, would be followed by an "Era of Peace" for the entire world.

The prophecies to the Fatima children were unprecedented. In 1930, the Church fully approved the events at Fatima. Most significantly, Mary's prophecy to the children regarding the spread of Communism (militant atheism) throughout the world, which was to be followed by an Era of Peace, was monumental. Indeed, some writers say that the events of Fatima are so significant that they can be compared with the way God led the Israelites out of Egypt. For

Fatima's "*new era*" is prophesied to be one that will again free God's people, just as the Israelites were set free from the slavery of Egypt. Only this time, God's people are to be set free, to a degree, from the spiritual slavery of sin.

In the same way that God had utilized a child at Lourdes to declare Mary's Immaculate Conception, the incredible announcements at Fatima were again delivered to the Church and to the world through the mouths of three poor shepherd children.

The Fatima visionaries were not to be the last children used by Heaven in this century. In numerous apparitions since Fatima, God has continued to use children as His mouthpieces.

The approved apparitions at Beauraing, Belgium in 1932-1933 were to five children, ranging in age from nine to fourteen. Likewise, twelve days after the Beauraing apparitions ended, twelve-year-old Mariette Beco began to see the Virgin Mary in the apparitions of Banneux, Belgium, which were also fully approved by the Church.

Numerous reported apparitions and visions throughout the 1940's, 50's, 60's and 70's continued to occur to visionaries who were children. The most celebrated were the reported apparitions of Mary to the four children at Garabandal, Spain (1961-1966). The visionaries were: Conchita Gonzalez, age twelve; Mari Loli Mason, age twelve; Mari Cruz Gonzalez, age eleven; and Jacinta Gonzalez, age twelve. These apparitions, like those at Fatima, were known for their incredible prophecies and outstanding supernatural characteristics, although they have not as yet been approved by the Church.

Since 1981, when six more children were chosen in Medjugorje, there have been literally dozens of reputable apparitions throughout the world. Not surprisingly, some of the most credible ones have been reportedly to children at places such as Oliveto Citra, Italy; Litmanova, Slovakia; Baghdad, Iraq; Kibeho, Africa; Hrushiv, Ukraine; Incheegela, Ireland and Terra Blanca, Mexico.

And this brings us back to little Audrey Santo. For in the lives of these chosen children, especially those of the twentieth century, a tapestry of individuals and events that are interwoven is unveiled.

Even Pope John Paul II, in his book, *Crossing the Threshold of Hope,* acknowledges this apparent truth (*"I could see there was a certain continuity among LaSallette, Lourdes and Fatima..."*).[10] Therefore, the lives of these children in Christ and their unique missions, and the fact that God felt with each of them a need to use them while they were still children, perhaps gives us a better basis from which to evaluate Audrey and her life.

Of course, each child is different and each mission uniquely divine. But since 1830 at Rue du Bac, Paris, the events and lives of God's chosen ones have shared a common thread. They have been called, it seems, to prepare the world for the end of one era and the beginning of the next. They have served as heroic examples of virtue and holiness. They have been prophets. Most of all, God has used each of them to bring unity, healing and peace and to help Him save souls. And once again, this is obviously the case with Audrey.

But with the prophecies at Fatima and later at Medjugorje, an additional factor came into the picture. The Virgin Mary declared that our times are dark and serious. She called the world to peace through conversion. And at Medjugorje, Mary even stated that this would be her **"last call"**, her **"last apparitions"**.

Most importantly, it must be remembered that at Fatima, the Virgin Mary revealed that God wished to save the world from *"annihilation"*. This is significant, as before the twentieth century, such a specific announcement had never been heard. But likewise, before this century, the world never had the power to completely destroy itself. Therefore, from Fatima until now, God's messages through Mary have contained a note of *"urgency"*.

Indeed, the Virgin repeats at Medjugorje and throughout the world that time is an important factor, as are prayer and penance. Mary has said that these are all critical ingredients in order for the **"triumph"** of the Immaculate Heart to come and to **"prevent"** the world from experiencing a great suffering.

Thus, if after two hundred years of heavenly warnings, and if the hour is as late as it seems, who better now than perhaps another chosen child to help respond to the urgency of the moment? An urgency said to especially require intercession and reparation ... as never before...

CHAPTER TWENTY-TWO

DANGEROUS TIMES

If Audrey's apparent mission of intercession and suffering is related to the Blessed Virgin Mary's warnings at Fatima and now at Medjugorje, then there can be no downplaying its gravity. Since Fatima's messages in 1917, Heaven has been attempting to alert the world that its sinful state could lead to a terrible moment of incomprehensible suffering.

Through words and visions, the great prophets of our time have reported seeing the heavens rain fire upon the earth. Over the last hundred years, dozens of mystics, stigmatists and visionaries have concurred that a great chastisement may come upon mankind. And these visionaries specifically emphasize that this tragedy will come from the "hands of men". The Church-approved apparitions of Akita, Japan in 1973 especially contain this urgent message, as Mary told the stigmatist, Sister Agnes Sasagawa, **"fire will fall from the sky and wipe out a greater part of humanity."**[1]

Since Fatima, numerous other messages, signs and warnings of this mounting danger have been given, including an incredible sign that occurred during the French testing of an atomic bomb in the Pacific in 1968.

Photographs of the nuclear explosion clearly show the undeniable image of Our Lord crucified on the cross in the center of the atomic mushroom cloud. To the right of Christ, there is a glowing all-white silhouette of Our Lady. This radiating image of Mary is distinctly visible in contrast with the background of the red mushroom cloud. It even appears to be the same likeness of Mary as Our Lady of Medjugorje! (Note: Upon closer examination using high contrast techniques, the photograph also appears to be somewhat of a replica of Sister Lucia's "Last Vision", given to her at Tuy, Spain in 1929."

Both *Newsweek* and *U.S. News & World Report* magazines published the photograph in the summer of 1989, with the latter disclosing a "secret" plan in the event of a nuclear war. This irony was not lost upon those who have pondered the contents of the unrevealed Third Secret of Fatima.

Most significantly, the messages of Fatima contain without question the most telling revelations of such a danger. Various Marian writers have pointed out how the October 13, 1917, miracle of the sun at Fatima and the January 25-26, 1938, aurora borealis over the northern sky (which Sister Lucia said was the "**great sign**" promised by Our Lady at Fatima) were both signs that carried an intrinsic prophetic warning of how "fire from the sky" could fall upon the world.

With mankind's all-out attack on life today through abortion, contraception, and euthanasia, the Virgin Mary continues to warn in her present-day apparitions that the world is drawing closer to this danger. Our Lady says that a fateful moment is drawing near because of these great sins against life itself. Indeed, Mother Teresa of Calcutta's words ring loudly and clearly, "The fruit of abortion is nuclear war."

Pope John Paul II alluded to this apparent reality in his October, 1987 visit to America, when he said, "The very condition of your survival as a nation depends on how you treat the weakest among you - those yet unborn in the womb."[2]

In Michael Brown's book, *The Final Hour*, Fr. Slavko Barbaric of Medjugorje said that the handwriting is on the wall as to what exactly the Virgin Mary is still trying to accomplish through her many intercessions in the world today. Stated Fr. Barbaric:

> The Madonna did not come to announce catastrophes, but more to help us avoid them. We all know nuclear war is possible, even without apparitions. If a house burns, it doesn't burn because the mother cries

"fire." On the contrary, the mother comes to save the house which is burning and in that there is hope.[3]

The events surrounding the life of little Audrey Santo are seen by her mother, Linda, her family and some priests to be connected to Mary's work at Fatima, and throughout the world at this time. They feel that God's justice is being appeased through Audrey's suffering and intercession.

While there are those who will immediately reject and disdain the idea that this suffering child may be tied to such a portentous theory as preventing world annihilation, one of Audrey's three spiritual directors is certainly convinced of the reality of such a view. He believes that Audrey is connected with the redemption of the sins of nuclear destruction. While highly controversial and extremely speculative, this is a view that is better served out in the open, where perhaps its merit can at least be debated, rather than ignored and someday found to have been carelessly overlooked and discarded.

Indeed, Fr. Emmanuel McCarthy, whose Peace and Justice Ministry has long studied the warnings found in Mary's apparitions and the profound, intrinsic meaning behind them, is convinced that Mary came to Fatima in 1917 to warn the world of the nuclear threat it would soon encounter. From studying numerous apparitions and historical Church and world events, Fr. Emmanuel is convinced that many of the signs the world has been given since Rue du Bac in 1830 have subtly alluded to, and sometimes boldly revealed, this highly mysterious scenario.

Fr. Emmanuel's convictions have been upheld through some of the events that surround little Audrey. For in her extraordinary life, he sees more signs of Heaven warning the world of the great danger it faces from nuclear weapons.

Most curiously, Fr. Emmanuel points out that official medical records show that Audrey Santo drowned in her backyard pool at 11:03 on August 9, 1987. And it was at 11:03 on August 9, 1945, that the United States dropped the second atomic bomb of World War II on Nagasaki, Japan. Like many other signs that have been given to the world as a warning of the danger of nuclear weapons, this coincidence should not be lightly dismissed. As occurred with Pope John Paul II's attempted assassination on May 13, 1981, the anniversary date of the first apparition at Fatima, God has repeatedly used coinciding "dates" as signs to alert His people. Pope John Paul has even stated that it was the "date" of his attempted assassination which awakened his awareness to the reality of Fatima's important message.

While it is difficult to examine this mystery in its entirety, Fr. Emmanuel revealed part of his understanding of what God has been trying to tell the world, as the Virgin Mary often warns, "before it is too late". Fr. Emmanuel explains:

Because the atomic bomb was dropped on Nagasaki on August 9th, this date has become a planetary date. Everyone in the world knows what happened on that date. But to get the full picture of what happened on that day it must be viewed with what happened on July 16, 1945, at Trinity Site in the New Mexico desert, the detonation of the first atomic bomb. For this date, like August 9th, is also a date that God has tried to use in order to draw our attention to the abyss into which humanity has dug itself - and to the way out of it, temporally and eternally.

On July 16, 1945, Robert Oppenheimer, who was the father of the atomic bomb and one of the greatest physicists of the century, said at the moment he saw the atomic explosion, "Now I have become death, the destroyer of worlds." This was an exact quote from the Hindu Scripture, Bhagavad-Gita. Oppenheimer instantly knew in his heart that he had moved the world in the wrong direction. This sentence, which he publicly acknowledges was his first thought, is the clearest of evidence that he was aware he had done something terrible. Here was a scientist that only a handful of people could talk to. He knew the depths of material reality in a way few people have understood them in the history of the world. Yet, the instant Oppenheimer saw the explosion, he knew that alterations of the subatomic and submolecular level had taken place that would inevitably lead to unthinkable destruction within humanity and within life in general. He understood how

141

things could get out of control, not just politically, but at submolecular dimensions of reality. These are the dimensions of reality that human beings could not yet understand but which effect literally everything else from viruses and bacteria to the climate and the air we breath. He knew that fundamental realities had been tampered with for destructive purposes and that destruction would follow.

What exactly has happened? When they started testing atomic bombs, it was thought you only had to be twenty miles away, downwind, to be safe. Then it was a hundred miles. Then, it was two hundred miles away to be safe. Today it is understood that the entire country east of any testing site is downwind and therefore in danger. "Why?", because the deadly effects of radiation are destructive beyond imagination - and beyond prevention. After an explosion, lethal radioactive material is carried out of the test site into the air, water, ground, animals, humans - wherever the wind blows. Thus, Oppenheimer was laserlike accurate in his initial thought. For destruction on a planetary scale had begun, though he didn't understand the details of it on July 16, 1945.

For example, St. George, Utah, which is downwind from a nuclear test site and had one of the lowest cancer rates in the United States before the nuclear testing began, has now one of the highest. You see, the terribleness of nuclear weapons, the destructiveness of nuclear weapons lies not exclusively in the people immediately killed, but also in the fact that the lethal consequences of these explosions immediately go into the entire world and effect untold numbers. Once again, what Oppenheimer thought, "I have become death, the destroyer of worlds," was the truth. Now, generations yet unborn, of human and nonhuman life, are being diseased and disfigured by processes of genetic mutation originating in these bombs, as well as, in chemical and bacteriological weapons.

Since 1945, we have exploded 1,900 nuclear

weapons on the continental U.S. The smallest explosion was on July 16, 1945. Many have been as much as 2,000 times more powerful than the original bomb. Russia has exploded 1,300 nuclear weapons, leaving in their trail the destruction of all forms of life through genetic alteration. In fact, the former Soviet city of Semipalatinsk is literally a graveyard and horror museum of people, animals and plants destroyed, diseased and disfigured by nuclear weapons - not by the explosions, but by the residual radiation effects. And so it goes with France, England, China, and India, all exploding nuclear weapons at test sites throughout the world. The entire world, to a degree only presently coming to light, is experiencing destruction from these bombs, as well as other weapons of mass destruction (chemical and bacteriological.) The entire world is downwind.

We must understand, that if we take the best minds in the world and employ them to learn how to ever more efficiently destroy life through weapons' technology, we will eventually bring down upon humanity a world where the living will envy the dead. The Biblical name for this is "judgment." Oppenheimer intuited it. But, how can we be saved from it? For we have put our time and our best minds into creating instruments of mass homicide. We have put our trust into defense by the sword. Thus, at the moment of crisis, which is now, we have no ability to respond except through more of the same - which response is literally and spiritually killing us. In other words, in choosing to defend ourselves in ways that Christ-God told us not to, we have ended up destroying ourselves. We are living amidst a lethal spiritual auto-immune disease where the means that we ourselves have chosen to protect ourselves are destroying us. On a smaller scale, but no less horrible, we see this diabolical dynamic playing itself out in the Gulf War Syndrome and in the 100,000 Vietnam Veterans suicides since the end of that war. It is a fatal error. Jesus warns us of it when He says, **"He who lives by the sword will perish by the sword."** It is the ultimate deception of

Satan to make people believe they can control evil once they have chosen it.

The atomic bombs detonated July 16, 1945, in New Mexico and on August 9, 1945, over Nagasaki, which by the way was the heart of Japanese Catholicism, were plutonium bombs. The bomb dropped on Hiroshima on August 6 was a uranium bomb. Uranium is deadly, but plutonium is the most deadly substance of earth. It gets its name from Pluto, the pagan god of the dead. It takes pounds of it to make a thermo-nuclear weapon. But, it takes only a speck of it to destroy or to alter irrevocably a human life. Just ponder the implications of the number of nuclear weapons that have been detonated to date! Judgment! An alcoholic does not become an alcoholic overnight. By the time the snakes finally come over the top of the bed at 3 a.m. to "devour" him or her in a delirium fit, he or she has been ignoring for years the truth that the person who lives by "the drink" will die by "the drink."

This is what has happened and is happening to our world where for thousands of years people have been destroying each other and preparing to destroy each other by ever more sophisticated weapons. Making weapons for human destruction is now the biggest business on the face of the earth. We have reached the final step of this diabolical journey across history because now our weapons end up destroying not just our enemy but our own people, animals, land as well as people, animals and land we are not even aware of. We end up creating new and horrible diseases. We end up destroying our own world and the worlds of countless other people in order to save ourselves or to save them! In short, humanity is now in a spiral of destruction that it cannot protect itself from. We have become helpless in the face of the consequences of our nuclear explosions -as well as decades of bacteriological and chemical experimentation. Therefore we have become "death, the destroyer of worlds" just as Oppenheimer thought to himself.

What all this means is that we are now either going

to be protected by God or we are not going to be protected at all. We have opened a nuclear Pandora's box. Yet we can still be saved from the consequence of our own evil because God is love, as well as the Lord of history. Long before this all began to occur, God saw the road humanity was going down, just as an objective observer can see the road an alcoholic, who is living in denial of his alcoholism, is taking. And so, God, who cares for us and loves us infinitely, began way back at Rue du Bac in 1830, to take steps through His loving mother, who is the Mother of Humanity, to save us from our own sinfulness.

At Rue du Bac, Paris, Mary brought the Miraculous Medal to begin to combat this danger. The medal is exactly what its name says it is - miraculous. For through this medal, the unexpected and the inexplicable began to occur to protect people. These were benign miraculous interventions of the power of God to fight Satan and to prevent the spiritual or physical destruction of human beings - and to let humanity know that the miraculous was possible.

Parenthetically, I think, it is important to say explicitly that Satan exists. Jesus tells us he is a liar and a murderer from the beginning. His perverted and perverting "personality" now desires only to destroy. Destroyer is his name. In God's plan of redemption, Mary has been combating the Satanic spirit on our behalf at least since the Annunciation. At La Salette, France, Mary's protective efforts on humanity's behalf continue with her intercession. This is also the case at Lourdes, where the last apparition to St. Bernadette occurs on July 16, 1858, the date which later would be the date of the first explosion of an atomic bomb in 1945, and which of course is the Feast of Our Lady of Mt. Carmel whose scapular is a symbol of protection in time and eternity. These are signs of the approaching danger, but they are also signs of God moving to save His people before they even know they need saving.

The apparition to the children of Pontmain, France

on January 17, 1871, is especially significant for seeing God sending Mary to combat the future danger of nuclear destruction. For at Pontmain, the people prayed the Rosary of the Twenty Six Martyrs of Nagasaki while they were watching the children (visionaries) in their encounter with Our Lady that night.

At Pontmain, the children said Our Lady held a red cross with a red corpus of Christ. This was totally unique in the history of apparitions and made no immediate sense. But years later, at Nagasaki, Dr. Takashi Nagai, a Catholic physican known as "The Gandhi of Japan" would tell how, on August 9, 1945 after he and others fled to a cave to survive the atomic bombing, human beings, who were skinned alive from head to toe by the atomic blast appeared at the entrance of the cave. These people were in mind-breaking pain and were completely red in color. They had, like the Christ (who) appeared on the cross at Pontmain, red bodies!

In addition at Pontmain, at the top of the cross that the children saw in the apparition, it did not read "INRI." Rather, it said just "Jesus Christ." Why did it say Jesus Christ? Well, Christ said, **"What you do to the least, you do to Me**." Therefore, in their suffering "red" bodies, we come to understand that the people - mostly Catholic - who were skinned alive by the atomic blast at Nagasaki resided in the suffering Christ and in a mystical way Christ was suffering in them, as He was suffering in those who were being persecuted by Saul to whom He said, **"Saul, Saul, why do you persecute Me?"** Finally it should be noted that the words of Our Lady at Pontmain were only one sentence, "My Son has heard your prayer." The next day the Prussian army stopped their advance through France just prior to reaching Pontmain and within a week the war ended.

At Fatima, we have an apparition of the Virgin Mary in which she comes as the Queen of the Most Holy Rosary. In the Rosary people have found protection for centuries. At Fatima, Mary "declares" that this is the prayer for protection. The Rosary is presented as

146

an instrument of protection from the snares of the satanic. Now it must be especially noted that Mary appeared at Fatima as Our Lady of Mt. Carmel with a rosary in her hand exactly when the 70,000 people at Fatima were witnessing the sun falling on them. In this, we find another sign of the coming danger - but also of protection. It is a scientific fact that upon detonation of an atomic bomb, the blast at its center is actually as hot as the surface of the sun. Later at Nagasaki and in Hiroshima, atomic bombs, whose explosions were to be as hot as the sun, came hurling out of the sky toward earth. Once again, Mary's appearance at Fatima at the moment when the sun fell from the sky was as Our Lady of Mt. Carmel whose feast day is July 16th, the anniversary of the first atomic bomb explosion.

But with each apparition, Mary has not only brought a warning in word or symbol of the coming dangers, but also instruments or means of help and protection. At Rue du Bac, it was the medal called miraculous. Belief in the miraculous requires belief in God and by extension in the power and wisdom of His way. It is brutally clear that human intellect left to itself will destroy humanity even if humanity at some future date is able to clone a world made up only of the "best and the brightest." The world is so ensnared, enmeshed and entangled in the viper's web of evil that it is impossible for humanity by its own resources to extricate itself from it. But what is impossible for human beings is possible for God. The unimaginably miraculous can save in time and in eternity. The Miraculous Medal communicated this unequivocally.

At Lourdes, on the day the healing spring was found, Mary asked Bernadette to eat a flower called saxifrage. While the people laughed at Bernadette, thinking she had lost her mind, there was, I believe, possibly a very serious reason for Our Lady's request that she eat this herb, if we assume that in an authentic apparition things aren't done arbitrarily and without purpose. This flower has medicinal qualities still being discovered.

Curiously it also is the same flower St. Therese of Lisieux's father handed her, when she told him she wished to enter the convent and he called her his "little flower." Is there help here that we are missing?

There was also a healing spring revealed at Banneux in 1933 where the Mother of God appeared under the title Virgin of the Poor, in biblical Hebrew, "Virgin of the Anawim." Consistent with God's love for all people and Jesus's desire to help and save all people, the visionary, Mariette Beco, was told by Mary that the spring was **"for all nations."** We can continue to see these signs of God's concern and love in many other apparitions, e.g. Knock, Ireland. But today we should especially note that Mary came to Medjugorje explicitly as the Queen of Peace.

At Medjugorje, Mary first appears on the sunny-side of the hill called Podbrdo. On the shadow side of that same hill there is a cliff where on August 6, 1941, three hundred Orthodox Christian men, women and children were slain by other Christians. Forty years to the day after this massacre, on August 6, 1981, the world "MIR" or "peace" appeared in the sky over Medjugorje. August 6th is, of course, also the anniversary of the first atomic bombing of Hiroshima in 1945. The significance of the Mother of God appearing under the title Queen of Peace at the end of this Century of Cain, in which more people have been killed in war than in all the centuries combined, should be self-evident. The significance of Our Lady appearing as Queen of Peace in former Yugoslavia where Orthodox and Catholics have been at each others throats for centuries should also be self-evident.

Most of all, these apparitions all tell us that the Gospel of Jesus Christ is the road to peace, the only road to authentic peace for all people. If Mary is the Queen of Peace the only peace she can be queen of is Christ's peace and the only way to that peace must be Christ's way, which is why her last words in the Gospel are, **"Do whatever He tells you."** Christians must make use of the graces that Mary brought to the world at Rue du Bac, Lourdes, Pontmain, Knock, Fatima, Banneux and Medjugorje to make peace in the world, to be peacemakers. For Christ is giving us the grace to bring peace to the world but we must "see with our eyes" the signs of the times, given to us through the Blessed Virgin, and accept wholeheartedly the truth to which they are pointing, namely, Jesus Christ and His Way.

So also, through Audrey, and through the unbegrudging love she receives, there is a communication to us as to how the Church, how all humanity, must go about making peace, being authentic peacemakers. How must we go about obtaining peace? We must go about it by serving one another through Christ-like love, as the Gospel says. We must be willing, like Linda does with Audrey, to suffer in our service for others. This is contrary to the worldly solutions and the worldly processes of peace. Remember, the A-bomb reportedly was made to bring us peace, but instead it brought suffering that continues to propagate itself throughout the world to this very hour. From Rue du Bac to Medjugorje, it seems what we have to do is ponder the infinite depth of it all - the signs, the dates, the messages - for if those apparitions are valid, they are an attempt by Christ-God to draw us back to His Way, which we have ignored or betrayed. They are an effort to empower us to love as Christ loves, to love what Christ loves and to reject what Christ rejects.

In Audrey's event, what is communicated is the heart of the Gospel. Section 1970 of the New Catechism of the Catholic Church proclaims: "The entire law of the Gospel is contained in the new commandment of Jesus to love one another as He loves us." (Jn. 13:34, Jn 15:12) The Audrey-event, as a reality and as a symbol, reveals to us how we are given a choice between the spirit of care and the spirit of destruction, between the Holy Spirit of love and the Satanic spirit of merciless indifference to human suffering. From abortion to atomic war, it is the spirits of destruction and merciless indifference to human pain that seem to rule the world - and to rule it under the lie that they are bringing peace. The world cries, "Peace!, Peace!" But, there is no peace. Why? **"If only you knew today the things that make for peace"** (Lk 19:41), says Jesus. The Audrey-event, like the apparitions from Rue du Bac to Medjugorje, point to what makes for peace and it is nothing other than Christ-like love. It is through the Christ-like love that permeates Audrey's reality that the world is being saved and not through the intrigues, violence and greed of those whom the world speaks well of. Who can believe it? Only those will believe it who believe that Christ on His cross is infinitely more powerful than Caesar on his throne.

According to some, there are more little oddities, more little signs, that indicate the connection between Audrey's suffering and what occurred at Nagasaki and Hiroshima. But the message remains the same. Like Mary's apparitions throughout the world today, Audrey's life in Christ and all the signs and wonders point toward the path to peace and away from destruction.

As Fr. Emmanuel noted, we must remember that the Virgin Mary came to Fatima and elsewhere to "prevent" destruction and to "convert" all of God's people. Indeed, her many intercessions on Fatima-related anniversary dates continue to remind us of this truth and to again confirm it to us.

In fact, even on the day the first atomic bomb was dropped on Hiroshima, this truth was especially noted as a group of priests survived at ground zero of the nuclear blast there. The priests later said that they survived because they were reciting the Fatima prayers. The same thing occurred at Nagasaki where a group of friars in the center of the city were found miraculously alive. Again, at Nagasaki, the friars said that their survival was due to their response to the requests of Our Lady of Fatima.

On July 16, 1990, Fr. Emmanuel, Linda Santo and several others, including Fr. George Zabelka, who was the Catholic chaplain for the Hiroshima and Nagasaki bomb crews in 1945, traveled to the Trinity site in New Mexico to pray on the anniversary of the first nuclear detonation there.

For twenty-four hours they prayed the Rosary, celebrated Mass and held a vigil in memory of what happened on July 16, 1945. All of this occurred in response to an inspiration Fr. Emmanuel had received while praying on Mt. Carmel in Israel, July 16, 1989. Since 1990, this prayer vigil has been repeated every July 16th. It now draws hundreds of participants each year who come to pray for peace.

In their video documentary on Audrey Santo, *Audrey's Life - Voice of a Silent Soul,* the Mercy Foundation of St. Louis, Missouri, summed up what they saw as the possible connection between the life and mission of Audrey Santo and the events at Nagasaki; they noted how both tragedies confront the value of human life. *"While one tragedy robbed humanity of its dignity,"* the narrator stated, *"the other has restored it."*[4]

Is the life and mission of little Audrey Santo connected to God's plan for the salvation of the world as revealed through Mary's apparitions over the last two centuries?

If so, it would be indeed ironic that, of all the children God has used to speak to us over the last two hundred years, this child's silent voice may be the loudest of all.

But this should not surprise us. In fact, even Pope John Paul II recently noted how powerfully God uses children. Remarking on the incredible and important ways God calls and utilizes the little ones, the Holy Father wrote in his December 13, 1994, *"Letter to the Children":*

> Think of St. Bernadette of Lourdes, the children of La Salette and in our own century, Lucia, Francisco and Jacinta of Fatima. Jesus and His Mother often choose children and give them important tasks for the life of the Church and of humanity... What enormous power the prayer of the children has!... IT IS TO YOUR PRAYERS, DEAR LITTLE FRIENDS, THAT I WANT TO ENTRUST THE PROBLEMS OF YOUR FAMILY AND OF ALL THE FAMILIES IN THE WORLD.

PART V

IN THE SERVICE OF LOVE

CHAPTER TWENTY-THREE

THE FINDINGS OF ABBE LAURENTIN

On some days, as many as a dozen priests come to visit little Audrey Santo. Her extraordinary life is now far from being a secret. In fact, the number of religious who journey to meet and "pray" with her is another "sign" of what God is doing through her.

As a discerning criterion, theologians often inquire whether or not priests and religious are drawn to an apparition or reported miraculous event. This, they say, is a strong indicator that the Holy Spirit is at work.

And indeed, Audrey Santo has attracted a significant number of priests and religious from all over the world. "*Over a thousand*," said Fr. John Meade. Observers say that Audrey even seems to have a unique relationship with priests. The nurses have noted how relaxed and happy she gets when they are with her, and how she squeezes their hands very hard. Likewise, God's chosen priest sons have many favorable things to say about Audrey and their experiences with her.

Noteworthy among the many priestly comments are the words of Fr. Daniel Gallagher of New England, an expert on mysticism who spent a considerable amount of time at the bedside of Marthe Robin (1902-1981). This famous French mystic was physically incapacitated, bedridden and blind for much of her life. Marthe

Robin, like Audrey, was a stigmatist. However, after observing Audrey, Fr. Gallagher commented, *"She is the greatest victim soul in the history of the Church."*

Fr. Edward McDonough, the renowned healing priest from Boston, is equally direct in his opinion of what God is doing through Audrey Santo. Fr. McDonough stated, *"You want to see the Church — go see Audrey."*

And Fr. John Meade noted that Audrey's suffering reminds him of Christ's Passion. Indeed, the life of Audrey Santo has made a tremendous impact on his own priesthood, and he has seen the same kind of impact on many of the priests who visit Audrey. *"Instant retreats,"* Fr. Meade said referring to the effect Audrey has on priests. Moreover, the suffering child seems to instill within them a profound realization regarding their vocation in Christ. Fr. Meade stated:

> All of a sudden it dawns on them. It changes them. It makes them take a step forward, closer to Christ. Priests come here skeptical and cynical and then have a tremendous experience as if it were a retreat of a week or two. They leave filled with belief, faith and trust – a trust in Divine Providence. They are on cloud nine. I've seen it happen many times. It's almost amusing. A thousand priests have been here. I have met priests from Ireland, Canada, England, India, Rome, and South America. We don't know how they find out about Audrey – all various ways. But it changes their lives.

While such statements may sound rash and extreme, the case of little Audrey Santo is so unique that it elicits strong opinions. Perhaps the Holy Spirit is moving these priests to speak without fear and trepidation. Fr. René Laurentin, who has authored over one hundred books, is a world-renowned Marian scholar. He is generally considered to be the most respected expert on Marian apparitions and mystical phenomena in the world today.

On two separate occasions, Fr. Laurentin traveled to Worcester, Massachusetts, to investigate the events surrounding Audrey Santo. Following is the second of his two reports. **(Note: This is an unedited translation of a report originally written in French.)**

156

THE LITTLE INNOCENT VICTIM OF WORCESTER, U.S.A.
(Second visit, 1995)
By Fr. René Laurentin

I published a first article about little Audrey Santo, this little girl, due to a medical error, who fell into a coma at the age of three years, and still lives with her family in Worcester. Her heroic pilgrimage to Medjugorje exhibited many signs. Since that time, Audrey assumes her state voluntarily, a victim soul, esteemed beyond words by those around her.

Previously, I had reported about the various signs according to witnesses, without having seen Audrey. But in the spiritual domain, as in the medical domain, direct knowledge is essential. I had hoped, then, to verify all this information personally.

When I arrived in Washington, Mr. Stan Karminski proposed to bring me to the Santo's home during the day of Saturday July 17, when I would be free. The trip would take place by private plane with my friend Dan Fannell, from morning to evening...

Linda Santo (Audrey's mother) was notified beforehand by phone, and soon arrived at the airport with one of her daughters, Audrey's sister. Both of them are short, dynamic and very friendly. They were Americans, very normal without pomp (filled with humility) and so authentic and kind-hearted, as is seldom experienced. This always reassures me when I visit places of mysterious significance. For if this is the case, what does the spiritual movement surrounding this small, comatose girl signify these past six years? How are they doing in this spiritual and material "knot of problems" which seems unsolvable? Why is this place becoming such a center for prayer and pilgrimage? "We live in a Jewish neighborhood," Linda stated during their trip from the airport toward her home. "We are the only Catholics. The Jewish people come also to pray near Audrey."

The (Santo) home is a wooden house with a modest exterior, comfortable interior and relatively large. The trip was well planned. They give me a dossier (folder) of documents. The family's spiritual director, the Reverend George V. Joyce who was not able to be present, left me a letter:

I can only speak of Audrey Santo with inadequacy...
The nurses' reports impressed me; signs of ecstasy

and of the stigmata. Hundreds of letters attest to the miracles and graces received through Audrey's intercession.

Conclusion: I only hold that she remains a mystery. Being her spiritual director for about two years, I know that she isn't only a beautiful child in a coma, but that she was especially chosen by Our Lord to give comfort to the sick and to bring back to His Sacred Heart vagabond souls.

Last night, a religious of the catechistic institute spontaneously reported an event analogous to Audrey's: A child at the age of eight years, Margaret Mary Ochenis, was stricken with a brain tumor, which necessitated surgery. She would suffer extreme pain, but she never would complain, as she continuously recited the Our Father. Each day, she would receive the Eucharist after she had received her First Communion. The doctors were astounded at her courage and her faith. She died in 1963 or 1964. "Nothing is more ignored than the sanctity of children," Daniel Ange thinks.

The dossier contained other witnesses concerning conversions and healings.

IN THE SANTO FAMILY

After one o'clock in the afternoon, I celebrated Holy Mass in the chapel within the house, in front of thirteen people of great and discrete fervor. For Audrey, they had asked me to break off a small piece of host, and to only give her a quarter of it. I thought of bringing it to her. But her mother who has the habit of doing this, took it from the altar. I rejoined her only afterward to give her the blessing.

After Holy Mass, Linda made me open the tabernacle. Within it is kept a host which is thought to be miraculous. On the 15th of January, 1992, when she (Linda) took this host from the tabernacle of Audrey's room to take a piece of it for the child, a piece of the host was blood-red. She kept the host. She (Linda) showed it to me. It is broken because of the few pieces taken from it for communion. I could see very well a stain which was vaguely red, but very pale. "The color is more or less vivid given certain days," the mother explained to me. The host was consecrated by the former Bishop on the 12th of January. Linda used it since Wednesday the 13th.

I prayed in front of Audrey who was laying on her bed. Her head was tilted on her side; her mouth was open; her head was strong for a child of her age; her hair is abundant like her sister's and combed with love, these long beautiful tresses of hair which don't have to be combed often, as she doesn't move frequently. She is an icon and an enigma. The family offered us lunch. But I ate little, worried that I would not take full advantage of the little time I had to better understand all that surrounds the large amount of fervor around this silent child within the sanctuary of her little room.

Audrey's eloquence is her lack of movement (immobility). Her dark eyes are very often wide open. There is a need for a permanent nurse next to Audrey, to watch for small accidents which can happen to someone who is immobile: breathing, etc. One of the three nurses on shift, Sonja Verta, short, but full of life, sparkling with large dark eyes, affected me with her fervent devotion for Audrey.

"They asked me to come to take care of her. I did not want to leave my family, my parents, four brothers and one sister. I prayed, I fasted, and I decided to come." The nurse has no regrets, as her whole being witnesses joy and a profound vitality. She objectively and clinically described, without commentary, what she observed and what struck her the most. During Lent, Audrey suffered more between twelve and three o'clock. During these hours, her body was more rigid, her head bent backwards and also her shoulders, her chest protruded up front, as if she were being crucified. Her pulse rose to 170 at certain times. This seems very high, she told me. When a person runs, it rises only to 120. During this time, the nurse was unable to lift her, as she was too heavy. She was not able to flex her arms. Her face turned toward the right. Her respiration became twice as rapid.

These phenomena were described to me in a note sent to me from Linda. Those familiar with Audrey see a connection to the Passion of Christ. (Without any literature) After this experience, at certain times, she (Audrey) seems to be clinically dead. It's as if her soul has left her body, as breathing seems almost nonexistent. Her face seems to be covered with wax. Afterward, the nurse says she must perform artificial respiration. The doctors come little, as they seem uninterested. She (the nurse) and others describe to me various characteristics and symptoms of stigmatists. The palm of the hand seems to split in two. Blood comes up from the stomach by the tube which serves to feed her. Audrey "attends" Holy Mass each day via the television. During the consecration, she enters into ecstasy: her head bent backward, eyes wide open, pupils facing upwards. The same thing happens when her spiritual director celebrates Holy Mass in her room. She (Audrey) received the Sacrament of the Sick in June, on the Feast of the Immaculate Heart of Mary. At that time, the doctor thought she would have only a few hours to live.

On May 5, 1992, Georgette, one of the three nurses who is not a Catholic but a Seventh Day Adventist, observed that on Audrey's forehead, there were nine drops of blood, which represented the crown of thorns. In the bedroom, I asked the other nurse, Joanne Erickson, who worked there for four years, "What is your work?"

"I give the medication," she said. "I perform physiotherapy, I supervise the cleaning of the respiratory tracts relating to the tracheotomy. And I give the doses of oxygen if it is needed."

"I did not want to observe the painful phenomena with the pulse rising to 200. Sometimes, the lungs fill with mucus, which needs to be removed." Sometimes, she (Joanne) would see drops of blood within the eye.

Two doctors are visiting in the room. One of them, Dr. John Harding, pediatrician, gives me his observations of the bloody host which was given to him to examine. "I recognized that there was blood, but I did not want to observe it under a microscope because of the respect I have for the Eucharist." Examination under a microscope would not have been disrespectful, I told him. But this was my impression.

The prolonging of Audrey's life, is it natural or supernatural? The doctor responded, "What surprises me is that there are no bedsores." Perhaps she has a special, electrified mattress? "No," he responded, "it is a regular mattress. In addition, people who are usually bedridden lose weight." She, however, is growing normally. Under the blankets, I could not perceive Audrey's body. I wondered to myself if her body had grown in the same proportion to her head which seemed large for her age. Her mother removed the blankets. Audrey has a normal weight and size. Her inactive legs, which have not moved since she was three years old, have no visible muscles.

Blood ran from Audrey's hands during Lent, Friday and Saturday, Linda assured me. "I saw crosses inscribe themselves on the back of the hand. Linda gave me some of Audrey's bandages, which oddly enough emitted an odor of roses," stated Dr. Harding.

The mother communicates with Audrey using the language of the eyes and of touch. Does Audrey speak with her hands? Not by gestures, but she can squeeze a hand which we give to her to hold.

Psychiatrist Dr. John Sears, who is near her bed, smiled at Audrey. He also seems to be communicating using his eyes. What he observed was that the skin of the palms seemed to disappear, only to reappear at his next visit.

Linda was also moved by the coincidence of dates. The accident took place on August 9th, the anniversary of the bombing of Nagasaki, exactly at the same time: eleven o'clock and three minutes (11:03). The 13th of October was the anniversary of the last apparition of the Blessed Mother at Fatima, when the physical therapist accidentally broke her legs. Audrey returned from the hospital on November 14, a date on which a bomb exploded some twenty years ago on the Basilica of Guadalupe. A priest friend of the family, who celebrates a yearly service in reparation for the dropping of the bomb at Nagasaki, seems to put a lot of weight on these coincidences.

RETURN FLIGHT

What is one to think of so many imponderable mysteries? This is what I ask myself upon entering the plane for my return flight, which received permission to descend to 1400 feet as we flew over the skyscrapers of Manhattan and the two Twin Towers which surpass 400 meters.

But these spectacular sights do not erase what I had just witnessed. As always, a religious phenomenon that is properly spiritual in nature, cannot be proven. God does not manifest Himself in a magical and public fashion, but through small signs (miracles), in obscurity, at times having meaning for those who believe, but insignificant for those without faith. The moving experience I witnessed is the fervor, the devotion, and the common conviction that the whole family shares: the children, the grandmother, the mother and the nurses.

Around Audrey, there reigns a union between all the inhabitants that attracts so many and radiates out to the community. Perhaps the phenomenon of Audrey is not technically miraculous, but it is certainly extraordinary. What a witness is seen within that house, with so much fervor, devotion, that it has become truly a center of pilgrimage for so many.

Every year, the anniversary of Audrey's accident is celebrated with a Holy Mass. The most striking feature of all of this is the tremendous love, a perfect entente within these difficult conditions of impossible life. The hospital has not corrected its error. But the many generosities of the admirable grandmother and of a few other individuals resolve the material problems, and especially a high quality of prayer, of understanding, and of mutual help, all cased by Audrey. This creates a beautiful climate of human and spiritual health. This is the most dominant aspect that I remember of my visit.

The stupidity of the medical accident and the unfortunate experience of the accident (at the pool) which was assumed by this woman (the mother) (whose husband left her) and her family with a faith and an extraordinary love of God which nourishes love of others, comes to fruition through healings and conversions. I will not describe these in detail, as they have not been the object of scientific statements.

Triumph of subjectivity, one would say, but subjectivity does not lastingly produce such an experience and such a radiation of love. My welcome has been completely simple and transparent. They showed me what I wanted to see with confidence. They invited me, without a doubt to partake, without trying to lead me astray. Is it not faith that saves? Yes, without a doubt, not in the sense of a psychological force, but in the sense that God performs His work, and makes real this beautiful union in a world that is often marked by division and separation. Yes, as Jesus stated, as also St. Paul specified, God much prefers weakness to strength. He much prefers humility to pride within this world. There, where hearts are responding to His call, He confounds the wisdom of the sages (wise) with folly in the eyes of the world. It is folly for a young, comatose girl to survive, to witness in her signs of a mysterious work of God through the enigma of silence. If this concert of love continues to grow through small daily signs of God's mysterious work, then they truly live with the Truth, those who have seized and understood one of these incomprehensible experiences which God has arisen today at the privileged place (this holy ground) for reparation of the sins of the world.

Jesus is the one who first did this for us. He also invited His mother to share in His pain. Audrey and those who surround her are a living sign of this eternal mystery. What God has realized by her unfortunate circumstances to be a source of healing for the world, we will only be able to understand this fully in the life to come!

René Laurentin

Audrey's room

Linda Santo in chapel
of Santo home.

*Oil dripping down
wall in chapel*

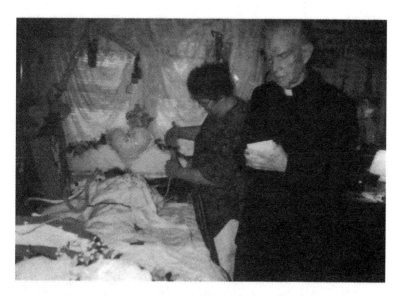

Fr. George Joyce at Audrey's bedside.

***Audrey's
Aunt,
Jerri Cox***

Msgr. Donato Conti of Rome with Jennifer.

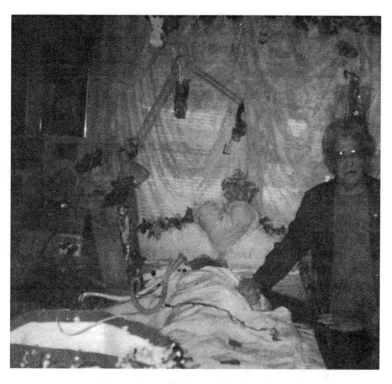

Grandma Nader with Audrey

*Miraculous manifestation of blood
on floor of tabernacle*

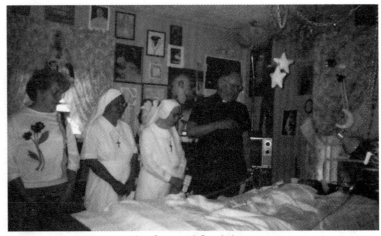

Audrey with visitors

Cabinet with relics and religious articles given to Audrey

*Several of the weeping
statues in Audrey's room.*

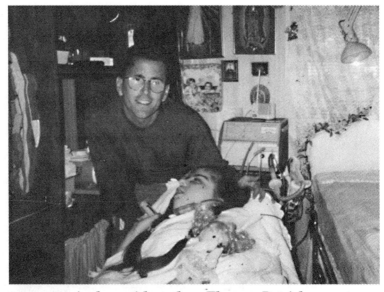

Audrey with author, Thomas Petrisko.

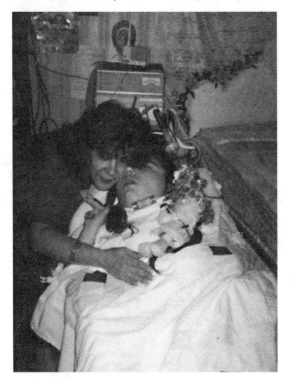

Linda and Audrey in Audrey's room.

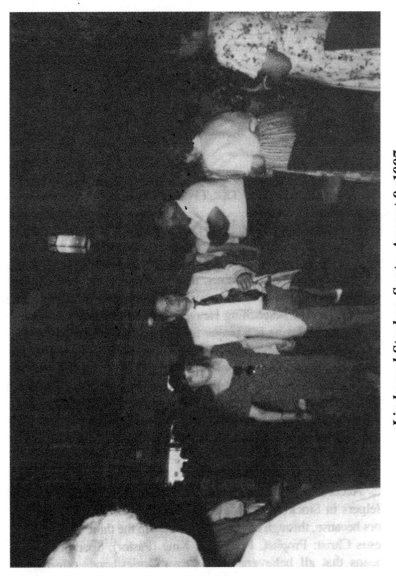

Linda and Stephen Santo, August 9, 1997

CHAPTER TWENTY-FOUR

BESEECHING HEAVEN

Many people believe that little Audrey Santo is a suffering servant in Christ. However, if indeed this is the case, Audrey
would also have to be an intercessor. For through her prayers and
suffering, she is beseeching Heaven on behalf of her fellow man.
In fact, her suffering is a prayer for others. This mystery surrounding Audrey is believed to have revealed itself even before her
apparent role as a victim soul.

But before we can understand what it means for a victim in
Christ to be an intercessor, we must first understand what an intercessor is and how the Church calls every member of the Body of
Christ to this very mission. Indeed, by our baptism alone, we are all
called to be intercessors.

According to Fr. George Kosicki, C.S.B., of the Marian
Helpers in Stockbridge, Massachusetts, all believers are intercessors because, through baptism, they share in the three-fold office of
Jesus Christ: Prophet, Priest and King (Pastor). Specifically, this
means that all believers are a "royal" priesthood, offering the
immaculate victim and themselves in the Eucharist for the salvation
of the world.

Jesus is the priest who lives forever and intercedes for all of
mankind now. Fr. Kosicki said this has been His role at the throne
of the Father for two thousand years. Moreover, it is Jesus who calls
us, the members of His Body, to participate with Him in this priestly work of intercession, for it is the source of our dignity as a royal

164

priesthood. Wrote Fr. Kosicki in his book, *Intercession*:

> We are a royal priesthood – we are intercessors with
> and in Him Who is the one Mediator before the Father.
> Sharing in His priesthood is not only a calling, it is also
> a duty. Because He has chosen and sanctified us, He
> wants us to cooperate with Him in His work of bringing
> salvation to all who approach God through Him (Heb
> 7:25 and 9:28). We have a duty to be intercessors with
> Him, before the Father, and so to be channels of His
> mercy to all.
>
> In practice, this means we are to be priests - always
> and everywhere, offering a sacrifice of thanks and
> praise, offering our whole created beings, that is our
> bodies, as a living sacrifice, holy and acceptable to God.
> It means that we are to be imitators of Christ who gave
> Himself for us out of love as an offering to God (Eph
> 5:1 and Jn 3:16) for all who believe.[1]

Not surprisingly, this is the teaching of the Church
as expressed in the Second Vatican Council:

> The baptized by regeneration and the anointing of
> the Holy Spirit are consecrated to be a spiritual house
> and a holy priesthood, that through all the works of
> Christian men they may offer spiritual sacrifices and
> proclaim the perfection of Him who called them out of
> darkness into His marvelous light (1 Pt 2:4-10).

According to the Church, to be an intercessor is to be one with
Christ. We are to be one priest, one body and one victim. We are to
be a living Eucharist, crying out to Heaven, "Father, behold Your
Son. Have mercy on us and on the whole world."

But it is especially "on the whole world," said Fr. Kosicki, that
our prayer of intercession is now so urgent, for he believes that the
present age is "*politically, economically, socially, ecologically and
spiritually*" on a collision course. Therefore, we need to intercede,
"*to intercede now!*" said Fr. Kosicki.[2]

Likewise, Pope John Paul II has echoed this urgent view of our
times most prophetically in his encyclical, *Dives in Misericordia*.
The Holy Father clearly recognized our need to intercede for God's
mercy on behalf of the whole world. Wrote the Holy Father:

...At no time and in no historical period - especially at a moment as critical as our own - can the Church forget the prayer that is a cry for the mercy of God amid the many forms of evil which weigh upon humanity and threaten it...

Let us have recourse to God through Christ, mindful of the words of Mary's Magnificat, which proclaim mercy "from generation to generation." Let us implore God's mercy for the present generation.[3]

Scripture teaches that in order to be an intercessor, there must be three dimensions to one's effort. First of all, one must act. Then, one must pray. Finally, one must make an offering.

But while we are all called to be intercessors, who among us is truly received by God as such? According to Scripture, when Christ called each of us to pick up our crosses and to follow Him, we were to follow in His footsteps through prayer and sacrifices. St. Paul wrote of this lesson to his followers:

Ever since we heard this (news of your growth in Christ) we have been praying for you unceasingly and asking that you may attain full knowledge of His will through perfect wisdom and spiritual insight (Col 1:9).

In this admonishment, Scripture is saying that as it was in the times of St. Paul, so it is now. True intercessors are those who sincerely discern a goal that only Heaven can fulfill.

Throughout Church history, there have been souls who have pleaded with God for the outpouring of His Holy Spirit, for the Kingdom of God, for mercy and for the Church. They have done this through many forms of prayer.

Theologians tell us that intercessors may plead spontaneously, or from prayers found in Scripture. Intercessors may recite the Psalms or the Rosary. They may even use the Our Father or the Chaplet of Mercy.

But most of all, true intercessors must unite their prayer with self-denial to add heart to their intercession. And for Catholics, prayers of intercession in union with the Eucharist or before the Blessed Sacrament are then perhaps the most intense form of supplication. These prayers actively direct the power of Christ's True Presence in the Sacrament toward the intercessor's pleas for divine assistance.

In addition, the motivating force behind all intercession must be love, because souls who respond to a God-given call to intercede on behalf of others are being led step by step down a path that God wants them travel. And it is only through love that they are able to do this. Love allows an individual to say "yes" to God, and love then permits him to take the action God desires. Truly then, it is the love of Christ which permits certain individuals to desire to do all they can for souls and for God.

Considering all of this, what kind of love and what kind of intercession are we speaking of as we attempt to understand God's motive and desires regarding the suffering life and intercessory prayers of Audrey Santo?

For if Audrey became a suffering servant in Christ at the age of four, and continues as such each and every day before the Blessed Sacrament, are we not indeed confronted by a mystical union resulting in intercessory capabilities beyond our wildest imagination?

Indeed, we can only ponder in awe what is perhaps occurring with Audrey's soul as a victim in Christ, united with Him on such a constant and unique basis of intercession. The totality of this divine scenario is incomprehensible; yet, it is all the more edifying and enlightening for us to ponder this magnificent scene, as Fr. Emmanuel noted, and there are even more factors to Audrey's intercessory capabilities that must be included in the picture.

Over the centuries, there have been many victim souls who have enjoyed the blessing of receiving spiritual Communions. That is, through profound meditation, these souls have experienced in vision the Holy Mass and the reception of the Sacred Species from afar. Such phenomena may occur in the lives of these chosen ones several times a day, which fulfills their constant yearning for spiritual union with the Lord.

On other occasions, some chosen souls have reported that they have received Communion in a miraculous way either from Our Lord, or from a saint or an angel. In fact, more than forty souls are documented as having received such a grace; sometimes, these chosen souls have exposed to public view the Host which miraculously appeared on their tongue. Once again, this is a grace bestowed on victim souls in order to satisfy and nourish them when, for some reason, they were unable to attend Mass to receive the Sacrament as usual.

But in the case of little Audrey, not only does she lay before the tabernacle each day, twenty four hours a day, but she has also received Holy Communion every day since she was five years old!

Therefore, with this additional fact, the enormity of the grace that is probably being bestowed upon her must be observed in greater detail. For if it is in and through the Eucharist, as Fr. Kosicki noted, that intercession is the most powerful, then what soul has ever adored and participated in Christ to the extent of little Audrey Santo?

The fact that Audrey is a child further compounds this mystery. For as such, she is sinless and pure, someone who is therefore able to offer God a special love devoid of any sensual confusion or material imperfection. All in all, it appears that Audrey's surrender to the cross would be almost perfect, and because of this, she may very well be raising a powerful voice before the Throne of God, the likes of which has never been heard before.

Moreover, proof of such a theory is growing. Since 1988, there have been many accounts from people who say that Audrey has successfully interceded on their behalf, as again and again prayers placed in Audrey's little hands have reportedly been answered.

Here are some of the many accounts forwarded on behalf of Audrey's intercession:

> - A sixteen year-old boy was healed of a form paralysis after his mother implored Audrey to pray for his healing and conversion. The boy answered the door the same day his mother returned home from praying at Audrey's house. He and his mother believe that he was healed through Audrey's direct assistance.

> - A woman who was unable to get pregnant for over ten years conceived the first month after asking for Audrey

to intercede for this intention.

- A young man immediately came out of coma after tears from Audrey's eyes were placed on him.

- A woman having a painful and difficult delivery progressed fine after talking to Audrey by phone. Meanwhile, Audrey's abdomen swelled and she appeared to begin heaving, as if taking the woman's condition upon herself.

- A woman with a tumor on her ovary came to see Audrey. Immediately afterward, the tumor disappeared while Audrey became symptomatic of the exact same condition.

- A woman visiting Audrey with multiple sclerosis let out a yell and fell to her knees. She reported that all her pain was suddenly gone. Meanwhile, Audrey simultaneously gasped as if in acute pain from a sudden affliction.

- Over a period of four months, Audrey's legs broke out in a bright red rash, which looked like a third degree burn. Following the requests of Audrey's pediatrician, a dermatologist took two biopsies of her legs and diagnosed "chemotherapy" burns. But Audrey has never had such chemotherapy. Meanwhile, the Santo family during this time began to receive a rash of reports of cancer healings of all sorts from around the country. The reports were from people who had been asking for little Audrey to intercede. (Note: In this case, the dermapathology report of Dr. Steven Franks of Westboro, Massachusetts was prepared by Skin Pathology Laboratory, Boston University School of Medicine, Boston, MA. The report states that "from June 24, 1994 through June 30, 1994, Audrey was officially diagnosed with hyperkeratosis of the acrosyringium and squamous metaplasia of eccrine ducts and eccrine glands consistent with syringosquamous metaplasia. Note: This condition has been reported in patients undergoing chemotherapy.")[4]

In addition, numerous reports of other "less critical" intercessory healings, including everything from arthritis to migraine headaches to fevers, have been registered with the Santo family. Often these reports are just letters of appreciation that do not specifically elaborate on what has occurred. The following letter, from a mother concerning her sick daughter, received in December, 1996, is an example.

> Dear Linda, little Audrey and Family,
>
> I hope that all is well with you and how's little Audrey? I tried to reach you. So I hope this card will reach you and let you know that the miracle I've asked the Lord through your daughter came true. She's recovered, is recovering and I hope fully recovered. You might not remember me with the thousands who come to visit you, but I'm that lady from New York who came to see you in 1994. Merry Christmas and I hope you will be able to let me know how little Audrey is doing. She's in my prayers every day.
>
> Sincerely,
Mary W. Alvarez
For my daughter Melanie
>
> P.S. Remember her also in your prayers.

Most mysterious, however, are the unknown and unrelated illnesses and conditions which Audrey appears to take on continually each day. Specifically, on different occasions and for short intervals, Audrey has appeared to suffer a host of maladies that her visitors bring to her. It is almost as if they drop off their sufferings at her doorstep, and she takes them upon herself with full knowledge of the consequences. While none of this can be proven, such "coincidental afflictions" continue to occur more often. For instance, in the summer of 1996, a child with cat-scratch fever visited Audrey, and one week later Audrey exhibited the symptoms of this disease. (Note: Audrey had no direct contact and was in a separate, secured room from this visitor.)

Likewise, on several occasions, mysterious ailments making the news somewhere in the world have also suddenly shown up in Audrey. The most memorable of these outbreaks was the strange E-coli bacterial infections that killed several Japanese youngsters and affected eight thousand more in the summer of 1996. This specific bacteria was then diagnosed in a sore on Audrey's neck several days after the outbreak.

But some of the most important healings occurring at the Santo home through little Audrey's prayers appear to be spiritual in nature. Conversions and reconciliations are always springing up. It has been especially remarkable how many people say that they have had their lives changed. Fr. John Meade said:

> Over the years, I think the greatest sign has been the reconciliations. During the annual anniversary Mass, where twenty to thirty priests consecrate together, the vast number of people go to confession. There are usually six to eight hundred people present and most of them go to confession that day. This is a tremendous sign of healing.

Is Audrey's capacity to intercede something more extraordinary than we can even begin to understand?

Indeed, some have said that Audrey's intercessory capacities have only just begun. And still a mystery is how Audrey receives these apparent sufferings, for not all of them are vocalized or read directly to her. Rather, like the saints who dwell with God in eternity and can apparently directly intercede for our petitions because of their closeness to God, Audrey is somehow receiving these sufferings above and beyond human communication.

Analyzing the unknown is no easy task, especially in trying to discern what God is doing through Audrey Santo. But Fr. René Laurentin, who has made a lifetime of analyzing such events, perhaps said it best when he concluded, *"Audrey remains a mystery, given her direct spiritual powers. I know that she is not just a beautiful child in a coma, but has been especially chosen by Our Lord to comfort and to heal and to lead wayward souls to His heart."*

Likewise, after a powerful personal experience with Audrey, Monsignor Donato Conti of the Vatican in Rome, who has visited Audrey on an annual basis for the last several years, maintained that *"Audrey is the greatest event in Church history."* Monsignor Conti has also personally briefed church authorities in Rome about the events unfolding around Audrey.

But surpassing all the mysteries surrounding little Audrey, yet another enigma surfaced in late 1994. While it is true that Audrey lays in her room before the Lord in the tabernacle twenty four hours a day, for some reason Heaven apparently decided to send another sign to help us ponder this reality in a more profound and deliberate fashion.

On March 28, 1995, an obvious red stain was noticed on a consecrated Host in the tabernacle in Audrey's bedroom. Significantly, this particular Host had been consecrated by the former Bishop of Worcester, Bishop Bernard Flanagan. And shortly thereafter, a laboratory analysis confirmed the suspicions: the red stain in the center of the Host was definitely *"human blood."*

CHAPTER TWENTY-FIVE

OVERWHELMED BY GOD'S MERCY

On four different occasions, consecrated Hosts in the Santo home have mysteriously changed in appearance and have begun to bleed. Likewise, brownish stains have been found on the white doily on the floor of the tabernacle in Audrey's room, and a red fluid has also been found in cups beneath a small crucifix in the chapel.

By 1995, the number of these kinds of events escalated. A red fluid was discovered at the base of a large crucifix in the chapel. A red substance was found outside the door of the tabernacle, inside on the tabernacle floor and down the left side of a chest.

Then, on May 22, 1996, upon raising the chalice during the consecration of the Mass, Fr. George Joyce, one of Audrey's spiritual directors, noticed that the chalice's base, as well as the paten, had mysteriously acquired a red substance.

Scientific experts were asked to investigate these unexplainable events. H.S. Research Laboratory of Cambridge, Massachusetts issued the following report on its analysis of the first of the bleeding Hosts.

H.S. RESEARCH LABORATORY
100 Inman St.
Cambridge, MA 02139
Telephone & Fax: 617-661-4370
REPORT ON PRELIMINARY INVESTIGATIONS OF

173

BLOODSTAIN WHICH APPEARED ON THE BLESSED SACRAMENT IN AUDREY SANTO'S ROOM ON MARCH 28, 1995

On Wednesday, March 29, 1995, I arrived at Audrey's home at about 11:45 a.m. Sometime after 1 p.m. Linda Santo, Audrey's mother, showed me and three Catholic priests present in Audrey's room the Blessed Sacrament which was kept in the tabernacle inside a gold-plated reliquary. This approximately one-inch size Host had an irregular stain of what appeared to me as blood occupying about half of the Host's surface. The stain on the Host was brownish similar to dried blood, but on the inside surface of the reliquary glass I could see a smear of what looked like fresh bright-red blood. After this visual observation, I decided to look at it under the microscope which I brought from my home. The idea was to examine the glass without touching the Host. However, when the back cover of the reliquary was opened and a ball of cotton which held the Host in place was removed, it was found that the Host was stuck to the glass. Not to destroy it, I just removed some cotton wool to which a tiny red spot was adhered. When moistened with physiological saline, the red spot appeared under the microscope as coagulated blood with red cells attached tightly to each other.

To demonstrate that this stain was really blood, the same piece of cotton ball was transferred from a microscopic slide to a reagent pad of a commercial kit for detection of occult blood. After adding a drop of developer, instantaneously a blue color developed which is indicative of the presence of blood. Five people who were witnessing all stages of these investigations placed their signatures on the reagent pad, which was wrapped in a plastic foil and placed in the tabernacle together with the Host secured in the reliquary. The whole process of investigations was also recorded on video tape.[1]

Boguslaw Lipinski, Ph.D.

Laboratory analyses on each occasion that an unknown red substance has appeared in the Santo home have been positive for the presence of human blood. Also, on different occasions, some Hosts within pyxes were discovered to have changed from their naturally hard composition to a soft and wet, almost "bubbly" texture. Fr. George Joyce remarked that one such Host felt "like tissue dissolved in water."

In early 1996, the miraculous presence of oil also began to occur more frequently. Then, out of nowhere on Wednesday, April 24, 1996, oil appeared on seventeen pages of the Sacramentary Book. These are the pages that contain the Eucharistic Prayers of the Mass.

On May 1st, several statues began weeping oil during Mass in the chapel. This phenomenon repeated itself on May 8th, as again statues wept oil and a miraculous odor of flowers was detected at the altar. On May 15th, not only did some statues weep oil, but this time oil miraculously appeared on the paten and on the Hosts during Mass. This phenomenon repeated itself two more times, not only in the chapel, but also in Audrey's room, once on May 22nd and again on May 29th.

Finally, on Wednesday June 5, 1996, as Mass was celebrated at the chapel of the Santo family home in Worcester, Massachusetts, another incredible miracle took place. Once again, everyone was awed.

On that day, three priests concelebrated the Mass: Fr. George Joyce, Fr. Tom McCarthy, C.S.V., of Chicago and Fr. Leo Potvin of Newport, New York. At the moment of the consecration, as Fr. Joyce elevated a large Host, he suddenly noticed that a smaller Host on the paten had changed color. When he examined the Host, Fr. Joyce found that there was blood in the center of the small Host.

A stunned silence filled the air. Indeed, the three priests were left shaken, and all in attendance were shocked. It undoubtedly appeared to be a Eucharistic miracle, and everyone knew it!

Fr. Tom McCarthy, recalling his feelings and thoughts at the time, said, "I was flabbergasted. I didn't know what to say. I didn't know what to do. But I knew a miracle was taking place."[2] Two priests from India were also present at the Mass. They, too, were left speechless. Fr. Bala Bachimala, who was interviewed right after the miracle for the documentary, *Audrey's Life*, said, "It was really touching...we were told these things happen here...but after seeing this personally, my faith has grown. I am touched."[3]

Out of respect for the diocese, the Santo family wishes that the bleeding Hosts not be called "Eucharistic miracles" unless the Church rules that it is so. But in light of the results from the laboratory tests, it has been hard to deny this apparent reality to the many faithful who come to the Santo home each week. Their hearts and souls hunger for the truth about these apparent miracles and about how they enhance the mysterious life and mission of Audrey Santo.

Like so many other Eucharistic miracles now being reported throughout the world, experts say that Heaven gives these signs both because of the lack of faith and God's infinite love for man. They are especially significant in light of recent surveys which reveal that only one-third of American Catholics believe in the Church's teaching on the doctrine of the True Presence of Christ in the Eucharist. So, Audrey's life and the events surrounding her seem to be very much oriented toward confronting the doubts of so many Catholics.

"It was primarily the Eucharistic message that we found here", said John Clote, President of the Mercy Foundation. "Our mission statement is very Eucharist-centered and we believe that that needs to be our central focus. We saw a tremendous amount of focus here on the Eucharist. We believe that Audrey is the vehicle that God is using to focus people's attention on Himself in the Eucharist."[4]

But even with the reported miracles, Fr. Emmanuel was quick to note an important fact concerning these mysterious Eucharistic events. Fr. Emmanuel said:

> We must remember that St. Thomas Aquinas noted that these types of events have nothing to do with transubstantiation. The consecrated Host is always fully the Body and Blood of Jesus Christ, whether there is any appearance of blood or not. Things like this can be happening, people drive miles or days for this type of miracle, when they can just go to their Church and receive Jesus in a Host.

While many clergy are not reluctant to offer their opinion in support of the mystical events surrounding little Audrey, perhaps the best source for testimony concerning these apparent Eucharistic miracles comes from Fr. George V. Joyce, the senior spiritual advisor to the Santo family.

Fr. Joyce is a diocesan priest from Washington, D.C., who retired in Springfield, Massachusetts. His almost daily interaction with Audrey Santo, and the incredible events surrounding her, validate him as a most credible expert witness to the events.

The following is an in-depth interview with Fr. Joyce. It is intended to present his findings and opinions based upon his subjective and objective experiences.

Q. *How long have you been involved with the events surrounding Audrey?*

A. Since 1991, approximately five years.

Q. *On Wednesday, June 5, 1996, there was apparently a Eucharistic miracle that occurred during Mass at approximately two o'clock in the afternoon at the Santo's home. You were the main celebrant of the Mass, along with Fr. McCarthy and Fr. Leo. Can you tell me what happened?*

A. We were into the Mass. I don't recall whether it occurred before the consecration or not. But I know that when I looked down in the consecration, I saw something that was not on top of the Host, but apparently was "in" the Host. So I sensed that something was going to happen. But, something had already happened so I went ahead with the consecration. And when I came to the "Behold the Lamb of God," I lifted the Host up and the first two rows of people said, "A-h-h!" I knew then something happened. I looked down and there was a small drop of blood on the Host.

Q. *What did the people say?*

A. The people in the first rows of the chapel gasped.

Q. *So, when you raised the Host up, these people had already seen the blood.*

A. Yes, they saw it on the large Host because it had rubbed off. The blood had rubbed off.

Q. *How many Hosts were there?*

A. There was a large Host and four small Hosts.

Q. *Was there blood on one of the small Hosts?*

A. There was. That's where the blood was concentrated.

Q. *Did the blood on the small Host rub onto the large Host?*

A. Yes, so that when I lifted the large Host up, it was on the side.

Q. *What else did you see?*

A. I looked down and I saw the small Host. The blood was concentrated on the center of the Host. The Host has a cross, you know, it has an indented cross in it. The blood was right where the beams met in the center. It (the flow of blood) was quite heavy - so the blood seeped out through the indentures of the cross as it were, you know, to the limbs of the cross and up above. I just looked at the Host today, and there is blood on both sides now. I mean it's penetrated. And there's a hole which you will see.

Q. *Did you consume that portion that had the blood on it?*

A. The three of us did, because we didn't pay attention at the time. We just consumed it. I took my share and then passed the rest over to the other two priests.

Q. *This was the fourth apparent Eucharistic miracle involving Audrey Santo?*

A. Yes, absolutely.

Q. *Was this the first apparent Eucharistic miracle in which you were presiding as the main celebrant of the Mass?*

A. This was the first miracle that happened at Mass. The other one, I consecrated and it was placed in the tabernacle in Audrey's room.

Q. *Was that the first or the second Host that bled?*

A. That was the second. We're talking about the second. That's the Host Audrey's mother, Linda gives her Communion from. She takes just a little fraction of a fragment and gives it to her. She (Linda) noticed it was darkening, just as the previous one, consecrated by Bishop Flanagan of Worcester.

Q. *Did the first Eucharistic miracle, the Host consecrated by Bishop Flanagan, the retired Bishop of Worcester, occur during a Mass or in the tabernacle?*

A. Again, it was similar. It was placed in a tabernacle and

then started changing.

Q. *Who first noticed that it changed?*

A. Linda (Santo) noticed it, and we didn't. It was very slight. t wasn't something we would all agree with. We thought it was a defect in the Host. But, Linda was sure it was something else. And it proved that she was right. It was blood and it burst forth one day.

Q. *Whose decision was it to have it tested?*

A. Fr. Meade and the Santo family.

Q. *Let's go back to the third miracle that occurred on June 5, 1996. What happened next? Describe what your thoughts were when you noticed that the Host had changed. What did you feel?*

A. You know, it's amazing because after the other bleeding Hosts, I'm just overwhelmed by God's mercy. I mean, I just have a great peace with it, which surprises me. Here I am seeing Jesus, the reality of the Eucharist, coming right out of my hand and right in front of me.

Q. *How does that make you feel as a priest? This kind of miracle has occurred to only a limited number of priests in history.*

A. It's not the honor of it, it's just the solidifying of my belief which has always been there, which again just fills my heart with joy because everything is confirmed.

Q. *There's a good point. This perhaps wasn't a miracle that was used to reinforce the faith of a doubting priest, as has occurred in some Eucharistic miracles. But the opposite occurred here, where it appears that the Lord was rewarding a priest who maintained his faith in Christ's True Presence.*

A. Yes, Jesus in the Eucharist is living. I mean, He's there! That's all you need to know!

Q. *What did the other priests at the Mass that day say when they were going through the experience?*

A. They were more overwhelmed because I've experienced the two miracles previously.

Q. *I understand one of the priests was crying.*

A. Fr. Tom McCarthy. He gave a little talk afterward and reviewed his experience in coming here. He first came here a couple of months ago. I believe a month ago, he saw the Our Lady of Guadalupe painting weeping oil profusely and he was touched. He was impressed. But he said he was not convinced when he went away. I mean, he wasn't overwhelmingly accepting everything he saw. But he was overwhelmed here. He had no doubts anymore and he was going to spread the news of Audrey and what's happening here. This is now!

Q. *Fr. Joyce, how did you first come to be exposed to the events surrounding Audrey Santo?*

A. I had just come back from Medjugorje and Audrey's grandmother was sitting here - Pat Nader. When I embraced her, I smelled the fragrance of Mary, which now I am familiar with. So I went and I saw this beautiful little girl, Audrey, with long beautiful hair in this strange coma, strange because her eyes were open. And I came away with a nice experience. I was feeling, you know, good about the whole thing. I felt the peace and the hospitality, their genuine appreciation of a priest visiting. I just sense that in this home.

Q. *What did you think of the events that occurred here before you came?*

A. Well, there wasn't much at that point.

Q. *Besides the apparent Eucharistic miracles, what else have you observed?*

A. They have records of people who have been healed and converted.

Q. *What do you think of Audrey's reported ability to intercede?*

A. These are miracles of mercy. So now's the time for Audrey. I mean, people will be attracted to her. I am convinced that it'll be more evident. People, I think, will walk out of here healed. We had a case last week where it was instant. It started at the consecration. It was at the consecration, that the healing occurred.

Q. *Father, let's talk about Audrey as a victim soul and the whole idea that a young girl, a child, would be introduced and asked by Our Lord to be a victim. Could you talk to us about that?*

A. Yes. Well, if I hadn't read in the history of the mystics that God calls souls, even very young, to this union, this mission of suffering, I wouldn't believe it. I think I would have walked away very skeptical. But that prepared me for Audrey. St. Catherine of Siena, at age six, saw a vision over the cathedral that started her in a mystical union with Christ. I read a book called, *The Stigmatists*, and there were other victim souls who were very young in it. But without that study, if I hadn't read it, it would be very mystifying. I don't fault anyone coming and going away saying, "She's a lovely girl, but I don't believe she's a victim." I mean, before all this happened, I'm speaking of before all the miracles happened, I wouldn't blame them. But now, of course, there's no question about it.

Q. *Father, how do you feel about the idea that in order for Audrey to be a victim, she had to say "yes" at some point, and perhaps at Medjugorje that moment came?*

A. Yes, I believe it. I believe it now. I believe it happened. That's apparent.

Q. *What do you believe happened?*

A. That at Medjugorje, she (Audrey Santo) said "yes" at one of the apparitions. That's what I perceived when I first came here. It could have been anywhere else. But that would be the logical place, because so much is happening over there. It seems that when Audrey was there for the last apparition, I think that was the moment that she accepted the victimhood from Our Lord and through Mary.

Q. *What do you make of the whole idea that this is in reparation for the sins in the world today, that Audrey is a victim who is offering reparation for the sins of the world today?*

A. Yes, Josyp Terelya, the Ukrainian visionary said it here last week. He said that she has suffered for the sins of mankind and now he believes she will get well as the world gets well spiritually. And that's how I feel too. I feel now that she will get well. I have no confirmation that would be logical. And I noticed the family agrees that she's not suffering apparently as she did before. It's the beginning of we'll say the "spiritual exodus" of what Our Lord wanted to happen here. The mission here is coming to a head. She's been effective for nine years. But the great thing that maybe God has in mind will come to pass. Because, it's such a buildup. It's overwhelming. A human mind must ask, "What is God going to do?" With all the oil and blood and the Eucharist? All this seems to be building up to some final mission that God has for Audrey.

Q. *You've been to Medjugorje how many times?*

A. I think thirteen.

Q. *Thirteen times. What do you make of all the apparitions and all the miracles and all the messages throughout the world, especially since Fatima in 1917?*

A. Our Lord is spelling it out. He spelled it out in the skies at Medjugorje. He wrote "MIR" in the sky. He is saying "I'M HERE". I believe the end times are here. This is occurring all over the world. God is pouring out His mercy, and His compassion, His healing. He is awakening souls. I've never seen so many souls suddenly awakening and dramatically coming to God because of a vision, visionary or reading a book.

Q. *With the Eucharistic miracles, do you think God is especially trying to call Catholics to the reality of the "True Presence"?*

A. Yes - absolutely - no question about it. We read about Julia Kim in Korea and the four children at Garabandal in the 1960's. There are miracles everywhere. These are very Eucharistic apparitions. We've seen the overwhelming presence of the Eucharist in all these apparitions. If a person really responds to the Eucharist, then everything falls in line. After looking at a Host bleeding, you should go home overwhelmed with the grace of the moment. And from the first to the last teaching of the Church - accept it as it comes. The miracles make it (the faith) alive and easily acceptable. I think it banishes all questions and doubts, you know. It humbles you to accept what the Church has been teaching. Even if we don't understand what is being taught, we cannot grasp and comprehend it,

182

but we must accept it.

Q. *Why do you think there is this great sign of so much oil here? Why are all the paintings and statues weeping oil?*

A. Well, Fr. Darius pointed out that in the pagan religious rituals, they used oil. And they used oil definitely in the Jewish ritual. There's always been oil. And Christ was called "The Anointed". Down through history, the Church used oil for centuries. Priests used it when ordained. When you're baptized, there's oil. When you're confirmed, there's oil. When you're married, there are some who bless with oil. We have always blessed with oil. I think it's simply a blessing and oil is a sign of healing.

Q. *What do you make of the people's responses here? What do you make of their reactions to Audrey, not just spiritually, but to actually seeing Audrey?*

A. They're all overwhelmed. Who wouldn't be to see so many statues, crucifixes, images weeping oil, weeping tears. Some pictures and statues have wept blood. Just recently, a couple of crosses, two or three crosses, shed blood. Then of course, the Eucharists are bleeding, which is high drama and finally their meeting Audrey. These people that come are, for the most part, very devout. You can see they're very devout. They respond wholeheartedly. It's a joy to look at them, because they understand what's going on, and it's just deepening their conversion. It's deepening their faith. I'm sure that some have been converted here, but as a whole, it's just confirming their faith.

Q. *What do you make of Audrey having intercessory powers? Reportedly through her intercession, there have been prayers answered.*

A. There's no question in my mind. God is confirming the fact that she is what has been claimed from the beginning, a victim soul. Otherwise, these things would not be happening.

Q. *So you're saying the intercessions confirm her victimhood?*

A. First of all, her victimhood would be from just looking at her. She's been mystically stricken. She's immobilized. She can't speak. That is, of course, a clear sign that she's suffering. And now take that, and all that has happened around her, which confirms her. Unless you or somebody can think of something else that she's doing? But obviously, all these years, she's been suffering quietly and silently for souls. There's a record here in the archives of healings, clear healings.

Q. *Can you tell us a little bit about the people's prayers being answered through Audrey's intercessions?*

A. The best proof is the records which have been kept. You know that many people are healed. For many people, miracles happen. For example, people take articles and they're on their way home and something happens. There was a sister who had a painting. She put it down and it was soaking (with) oil. I think the records are in there. That's the only thing you could say. For the critical world, you'd have to say, "Well, here's what this person wrote in the records and she was healed." What I think is going to happen, is from now on you're going to have more clear, instant healings. The first sign of that was last week. This lady with multiple sclerosis was here. She gave her testimony. At the consecration of the Mass, all her pain left her. Then, when she was in the side room looking at Audrey, she was "slain in the Spirit." At that moment, Audrey went into a kind of spasm, which is a sign that she may have taken on this lady's multiple sclerosis. On another occasion, her legs changed colors as if from chemotherapy burns. I saw her (Audrey's) legs. Did you hear about the legs? Well, it was as if every vein in her body burst. They were just absolutely red inside, and the doctors said the only thing that they know (would cause it) is an overdose of chemotherapy. So, very likely, that went on for about two weeks.

Q. *Have you seen signs of when she's in ecstasy?*

A. Yes, you can see it in her eyes. They won't blink. You can wave your hand in front of her eyes, and you can tell she's in ecstasy.

Q. *Have you witnessed Audrey bleeding?*

A. Yes, it's quite unique in that here is a little girl that people could come, look at, and say "She's a lovely girl. They say she's a 'victim'. But - no, I don't believe." But as I said, I wouldn't fault them, because there wasn't any real evidence at first. But what really impressed me were the two dabs of blood - one from her right hand and one from her left hand.

Q. *How would you summarize all of this?*

A. To me, God finally said: *"Yes, she is my victim,"* when all these wonderful miracles took place. They confirmed to me, that she is what the family and others believed for quite a while - a victim soul in Christ.

CHAPTER TWENTY-SIX

TRULY PRESENT

Fatima. Once again we must look to Fatima in order to understand Fr. Joyce's reflections on the urgency of our times and the desperate need for mercy, and especially why and how the miraculous events surrounding little Audrey Santo appear to be an urgent call to the Eucharist.

At Fatima, the Church and the world received an illuminating grace. It is a grace that permits us to look backward and forward at the same time. Indeed, many writers say that Fatima serves as a bellwether moment in Christian history. Through the Virgin Mary's revelations there, the Church was given for the first time in two thousand years a defining Heavenly perspective regarding where it was and where God wanted to take it. According to the experts, this perspective, given through Mary's words at Fatima, is invaluable to understanding the prophetic message of the Gospels, which promise Christ's inevitable victory.

In his book, *Crossing the Threshold of Hope,* Pope John Paul II wrote of his own understanding of this reality in the message of Fatima, how he came to this understanding and its significance in human history. Wrote the Holy Father:

> After my election as Pope, as I became more involved in the problems of the universal Church, I came to have a similar conviction: on this universal level, if victory comes, it will be brought by Mary.

186

Christ will conquer through her, because He wants the Church's victories now and in the future to be linked to her.

I held this conviction even though I did not yet know very much about Fatima. I could see, however, that there was a certain continuity among La Salette, Lourdes and Fatima - and, in the distant past, our Polish Jasna Gora.

And thus we come to May 13, 1981, when I was wounded by gunshots fired in St. Peter's Square. At first, I did not pay attention to the fact that the assassination attempt had occurred on the exact anniversary of the day Mary appeared to the three children at Fatima in Portugal and spoke to them the words that now, at the end of this century, seem to be close to their fulfillment.[1]

"The words", as the Pope stated, that are now close to fulfillment are Heaven's words of hope which Mary left at Fatima. Most specifically, the Pope is referring to Mary's words that promised **"an Era of Peace"** which would come into the world. It is an era that the Holy Father believes we will see at the end of the twentieth century.

But at Fatima, in addition to all that Mary promised in her messages, Heaven was also trying to say from the onset of the Fatima apparitions that the quickest and safest path to this peace lay not in Mary's words, but in man's coming to fully accept and utilize Christ's True Presence in the Eucharist.

Indeed, it must be emphasized how Fatima's message can be synthesized and reduced to one simple solution which would bring peace into the world: Christ, the Innocent Lamb, left us His Body and Blood to eat, in order to give us life, so that He may live in us and we in Him. And if we partake of Him, then indeed the Era of Sin will give way to the promised Era of Peace. It will be a peace based upon our secure knowledge of Christ's True Presence. Hence, the Eucharistic emphasis of the message of Fatima is much more revealing of the future than even Fatima's incredible prophecies.

Moreover, the depth of Fatima's Eucharistic call cannot be found in just the Fatima prayers, nor in the apparitions and their revelations. Rather, if we look closely, we will find that much more was given to us, and it was given right from the very beginning of the events at Fatima.

At Fatima, the Eucharist was of such great significance to Mary's message that Mary's first apparition took place on May 13, 1917, the Feast of Our Lady of the Blessed Sacrament at that time.

Years later, after the publication of Sister Lucia's memoirs, theologians began to understand the deep meaning of this occurrence. This "sign" underscored how much God wanted His people to come to a better and deeper understanding of the True Presence of Jesus in the Eucharist.

But there is much more. Many experts say that the Eucharistic message of Fatima appears to be a message for the Church that was designed by God to preempt the approaching times of duress, especially the times in which we now live. Heaven knew that these times would hold great confusion for the Church, especially concerning Eucharistic adoration and Eucharistic reparation.

While Vatican II placed great emphasis on the priority of the Mass, an unforeseen result was the placement of the tabernacle to one side of the Church. Many initially understood this to be a de-emphasis of Eucharistic adoration. But in reality, the Council was attempting to create special chapels of adoration. Fortunately, this situation was rectified to a degree through the efforts of many Fatima apostolates, which recognized that the Fatima apparitions revealed Heaven's desire for Eucharistic adoration.

In the 1916 apparition of the angel to the three children at Fatima, the prostration of the angel before the Blessed Sacrament was one indication. Then, with Mary's first apparition, the children themselves fell to the ground in adoration before a beam of streaming light in which they "recognized and felt lost in God." The children then repeated the angel's words to them in reparation for offenses against the Eucharist. Theologians say that this again was especially designed to emphasize Christ's True Presence in the Sacrament.

Likewise, adoration of the Eucharist as an emphasis of Fatima's message was revealed through Jacinta's words, which relayed Our Lady's request for a chapel of perpetual adoration in the Cova da Iria. This chapel stands today just a short distance from where the Virgin appeared, and millions of believers over the decades have adored the Lord there. In fact, it is recognized by some as the faithful's response to Our Lord's words at Gethsemane: **"Could you not watch one hour with Me?"** (Mt 26:40). Some believe that Our Lady prepared the children at Fatima in imitation of her own earthly way after the Lord's Ascension. Along with the Apostles, Mary is believed to have become a model of Eucharistic love as she spent her remaining years particularly close to the Blessed Sacrament. St. Peter Julian Eymard wrote, "Mary found again in the adorable Host, the blessed fruit of her womb. She ascended Calvary, but she returned with her adopted son, St. John, to begin in the Cenacle her new maternity at the feet of Jesus in the Eucharist."

Through Our Lady's many intercessions and apparitions today, Heaven continues to send her to teach and guide her children in accepting the truth of her Son's True Presence in the Eucharist, and to show them how to adore Him there. Mary's words in so many of her messages reveal this teaching which she obviously feels is of the highest importance for her earthly children.

In fact, when Mary opened her hands over the three children at Fatima and poured upon them the Eucharistic light, some writers that say Our Lady was duplicating in a mystical way the moment she first brought forth her Son into this world in Bethlehem. From her flesh, Christ would redeem us and then nourish us in the Eucharist, and all of this began that first night through Mary's Immaculate Heart.

At Fatima, the significance of this is reenacted every October 12th, as thousands adore the Blessed Sacrament in all-night adoration before Fatima's annual celebration the next day. The celebration then shifts to Mary and reveals the truth of her words at Fatima: **"God wishes to establish in the world devotion to my Immaculate Heart."**

Along with Fatima's call to Eucharistic adoration, there was also a strong appeal to the faithful for Eucharistic reparation. This is seen in many of the statements attributed to the children. But theologians say that Sister Lucia's climactic vision at Tuy, Spain in 1929, of a crucified Christ being offered to the Eternal Father, was an especially important sign from Fatima of God's call to

Eucharistic reparation. This vision, known as the Last Vision, carried great mystical significance, especially Sister Lucia's vivid description of both Christ crucified and the Host dripping blood into the chalice on the altar below.

With this vision, Heaven seemed to be revealing that Christ's sacrifice on Calvary is mystically continued through the Mass. Thus, the Last Vision corroborates almost perfectly the Church's declarations at the Council of Trent and Vatican II concerning the true meaning of the Holy Sacrifice of the Mass.

From the Last Vision we are called to understand that at Mass, we too, like Mary, are to offer ourselves in union with Christ in reparation for the sins of mankind. Like the children of Fatima, with the reception of each Holy Communion, we can offer reparation for sacrilegious Communions, desecrated tabernacles and the many violations of consecrated hosts which have occurred over the centuries. With our offering, we too are doing what the angel asked the children of Fatima: "Receive the Body and Blood of Our Lord Jesus Christ, horribly outraged by ungrateful men."

All of this again relates to the life and mission of little Audrey. For twenty-four hours a day, seven days a week, fifty two weeks a year, little Audrey Santo lays in her room in front of a tabernacle that holds the True Presence of Our Lord, a presence that has on four occasions apparently manifested itself in a most powerful and visible way. Her adoration and reparation is vigilant.

But like the Last Vision, which several artists have painted in an attempt to convey the powerful Eucharistic image shown to Sister Lucia, a permanent and perhaps worldwide Eucharistic call has emerged from the events surrounding little Audrey. This "miracle", like the paintings of Sister Lucia's Last Vision, will apparently serve as a visual catalyst for Heaven's call to the Eucharist during our troubled times.

On June 5, 1996, the apparent Eucharistic miracle that occurred during the Mass at the Santo home was not only witnessed by a couple dozen amazed people, but was also captured on video by the Mercy Foundation of St. Louis.

This professional film company was at the Santo home to film the documentary, *Audrey's Life*. Since the documentary centered around the call to the Eucharist that has emerged in the events surrounding little Audrey, the producers wanted to film one of the weekly Masses held at the Santo home. Thus, they were in the process of filming the entire Mass that day for the documentary, when the Eucharistic miracle occurred. According to some experts, never before has such a miracle been videotaped. Consequently, perhaps the importance of this miraculous event has yet to be realized.

Daniel Lynch, a Vermont attorney, judge and National Guardian of the Missionary Image of Our Lady of Guadalupe, offered his opinion on the significance of what occurred that day before the cameras. Said Mr. Lynch:

> In the history of the world, perhaps a few hundred or thousand people have ever witnessed a Eucharistic miracle. Now, with this miracle being caught on film, millions and millions will see it. Just the looks on the priests' faces are priceless. You can see how astonished they were. In a way, this "filming" of the Eucharistic miracle was just as miraculous.

Indeed, John Clote, the President and Founder of the Mercy Foundation, an organization dedicated to spreading the Virgin Mary's message of mercy and to promoting Eucharistic adoration, could not believe what occurred before his very eyes while filming the documentary. Said Mr. Clote:

> The last thing in the world we expected was to see a Eucharistic miracle but that is, in fact, what happened. Fr. Joyce raised the Host at the consecration, as in any normal Mass, and said the words of consecration. Then, the Host immediately became a very dark red color in the center. It seemed to be sopping with blood. We have pictures of that. It's recorded on tape. Our cameraman was so overwhelmed by it that he began crying. We changed the battery real quick on the camera and started rolling again. It was an incredible moment.[2]

Most significantly, if such miracles are indeed so extremely rare, what importance does this particular Eucharistic miracle carry? And why has another extraordinary Eucharistic event occurred around the suffering Audrey? Was the apparent Eucharistic miracle captured on film intended by Heaven as another Last Vision for us to contemplate? Certainly, no one really knows for sure.

But as Fr. Emmanuel has stated, "We must ponder what God gives us, in order to obtain peace."

CHAPTER TWENTY-SEVEN

A LIVING, BREATHING
TESTIMONY FOR LIFE

A udrey had been home for only days when a man uttered for
some unknown reason, *"Pray for me, little Audrey."* In retrospect, this was an extraordinary statement, if not prophetic. But
what prompted this man to utter such profound words?

At the time, there were no definitive signs that Audrey's life
possessed a divine mission. There were no bleeding or weeping
statues, no scent of roses or miraculous Hosts, and no healings or
conversions. Yet, this one individual uttered an incredible statement
from his heart - a statement that undoubtedly must have been
inspired by God.

Indeed, the Holy Spirit moved, and the faithful received a gift.
Little Audrey Santo's apparent mission of intercession and reparation was beginning. And the Church's Mystical Body intuitively
embraced her future role, as God appears to have directed this humble beginning through a casual utterance from another "chosen
soul".

Throughout Church history, many stories abound regarding
how great saints mysteriously arose from obscurity after the benign
utterances of a few individuals. As in Audrey's case, it often began
when the faithful recognized a life of holiness, and then upon death,

people would beseech the godly soul for assistance. Soon after, prayers were found to have been answered. And then, upon thorough Church investigation, it became evident that one more soul stood before the throne of God ready to assist the Church Militant.

The most remarkable cases were those that emerged from out of nowhere. These are the stories of saintly souls who went about their earthly existence in such an obedient manner that their humility completely masked their divine guidance. Often they lived in such a way that Church officials, or even their next-door neighbors, were unable to recognize how virtuous they had become.

St. John Neumann was such a saint. His public struggles as a priest led him from Bavaria through New York, Buffalo, Pittsburgh, Baltimore and finally to Philadelphia, where he was ordained a bishop. He died there before his fiftieth birthday.

Yet upon his death, reports of people praying to him were greeted with shock by Church officials. Soon, however, miracles were being attributed to his intercession, as onlookers finally learned what Heaven knew all along.

Similar is the story of Fr. Solanus Casey, a Capuchin priest from Detroit who died in 1957. His humble, hidden life, sometimes as a lowly doorkeeper, was outwardly unremarkable. Yet upon his death, people immediately began to call upon him as an intercessor for their needs. This again flabbergasted Church officials, and was something that only the Holy Spirit could have initiated. Today, Fr. Solanus Casey's life stands before the Congregation for the Causes of Saints.

But while it is one thing to recognize the Holy Spirit inspiring devotion to a deceased soul whose life was heroic and virtuous, it is certainly another to attempt to understand this kind of action in the case of a living person. Indeed, the entire idea may be disturbing to some and even irreverent to others. Of course, there must be caution. Audrey Santo's life is still unfolding, and no one knows for sure what exactly will happen with and through her.

Yet, at the same time, Audrey cannot speak to answer our questions. And in view of the holy and miraculous events that have emerged since her accident, it is logical to suspect that, prompted by the Holy Spirit, one man was inspired to request Audrey's prayers, thereby forwarding God's plan.

Most importantly, while God may conceal from us the full understanding of Audrey's mission, this does not mean that He wants us to withdraw and avoid the mystery. If indeed God intended to use Audrey in such a powerful way, it had to be revealed to the faithful sooner or later. And though questions remain, it appears that the faithful are nonetheless being invited by the Spirit to respond with trust and confidence. For refusing to respond merely due to a lack of understanding could thwart God's very purpose, thus perhaps wasting His gifts because of fear and ignorance.

Therefore, *"Pray for me, little Audrey"* becomes an urgent battle cry for the faithful. For through the life of Audrey Santo, we are called to consider that she may be someone God wishes us to turn to in our desperate times.

But just in her mere life and her remarkable state of existence, we also find as powerful a message to us from God as we do in the many miracles which surround her. For as many priests have noted, the truly profound meaning of Audrey's mission does not lie in the many supernatural events. Rather, it lies in her very life, in her fragile, helpless existence.

Moreover, in our distorted world, where the sacredness of human life is eroded more and more each day, God perhaps seeks to reveal through Audrey how very meaningful just one helpless life can be, and how important it is in the eyes of God. This appears to be something we all have lost touch with to some degree or another.

Thus, God is clearly showing us through Audrey that He has a purpose for every life, for every soul. And regardless of how helpless and insignificant a life may seem in the eyes of men, God's ways are not our ways. Each life is conceived in His mind with meaning and purpose. No life is without significance, and certainly this is what God has always tried to convey to us throughout Scripture.

Unfortunately, though, our age and times have sought to deny Scripture's message. We have become our own gods. In our small yet pride-filled minds, we have taken upon ourselves not only to become the masters of our world, but also the authors of the very meaning of life. As a result, instead of treasuring the greatest of all gifts, we have reduced life's significance, and then proceeded to discard it as if it were just another material possession.

Beyond the horrors of war and murder, through birth control, abortion, infanticide, and euthanasia, men now actively destroy life without remorse or regret. What can be seen and heard, what is useful and beneficial by worldly standards, has become all that matters. What cannot be seen and heard, what is not "functional" or "personally rewarding" is deemed insignificant in our world. Therefore, it is also discarded for those same reasons.

Helpless, speechless, and only a child, Audrey's human condition confronts us with society's love affair with abortion. Indeed, Audrey's dependent state accurately parallels the helplessness of the unborn. Like the unborn child, sacrifices must be made to take care of Audrey at the cost of quality of life, and surveys repeatedly show that "quality of life" is the primary cause of abortion.

The same is true for many of the elderly, deemed to have no future capability to "positively contribute" to society. For many of these so-called "worthless elderly", all that remains is their need for life's basic essentials. Likewise, Audrey's bed-confined, medically-supported existence outwardly reveals only the constant demand she will make upon the system that must support her.

Therefore, in the life of Audrey Santo, the unseen and unheard child in the womb and the ninety-five-year-old incapacitated Alzheimer patient blur into one. They are lives that the world finds questionable in either their true existence or real usefulness; lives that the world would like to ignore; they are also lives that become susceptible to a political process which seeks to determine who lives and who doesn't.

With society's unsacred opinion toward such helpless individuals come the unstable parameters of such beliefs. For indeed, the door opens wide for the eventual discarding of not just the unborn and the elderly, but also numerous categories of potential victims, whose human conditions leave them in equally vulnerable states.

Thus, from the mentally retarded to those such as AIDS patients whose very survival is a drain on "the system", all life is now potentially at risk. And with this reality, we may now be headed down the darkest road of all, the road to hell on earth, where every life may have to prove its worth in order to merit existence.

Impossible? Such evil will never fully manifest itself? Those who respond in such a way offer few guarantees and are oblivious to the spiritual dimension that drives the age-old confrontation between good and evil. For with the right conditions, all inhuman acts of genocide can develop into fair game and become tolerable. Remember that in the thirty years since the U.S. Supreme Court upheld the legalization of abortion in America, over 35 million babies have been murdered in their mothers' wombs. Likewise, the same nightmare with euthanasia may be on the verge of occurring.

In the Netherlands, a country of 15 million people where euthanasia is legal, nearly 12,000 people were euthanized in 1990 alone. And fifty percent of these deaths occurred without the person's consent. An additional 13,500 people were denied life-saving treatment, a practice the Dutch call "euthanasia by commission". Applied to a nation the size of the United States, this figure would account for almost 500,000 deaths a year through both forms of euthanasia. The Dutch themselves say that they never expected euthanasia to be so widely practiced. But it is. And in America, this holocaust would probably be unfathomable in size, as experts already note how abuses would rapidly take hold.

The life of little Audrey Santo illustrates every layer of the profound question of who lives and who dies. For Audrey's life reflects the reality of our dilemma over the meaning and value of life. As Fr. Emmanuel asserted, *"The reality is this, either all life is sacred or all life is meaningless. Either we are made in the image and likeness of God or we are not..."*

Indeed, and God's answer has already been given. He has apparently chosen to teach the world a lesson through the life of one helpless, silent little girl. Through Audrey's life and suffering, through her confined and restricted existence, God is showing us that every life, no matter how helpless and useless in the eyes of the world, has a purpose and is infinitely valuable.

Audrey's life was saved despite the accident, and although she remains as helpless as an unborn child and as confined as a disabled senior citizen, God has demonstrated to us through many miracles that He is using her to convert souls, to unite people and to bring healing. Therefore, this broken, silent child becomes a most noble, heroic and valuable servant to God and to her fellow man. She is proving beyond a doubt that every life has an infinite, invisible value, just as Scripture reveals.

But most importantly, through Audrey's life, we are specifically shown the ultimate message of the Gospel: *the call to love*. We are to unconditionally give and receive love as Audrey Santo does. There is no judging in her. And the greatest benefit to our lives from her life comes through faith. With this, the Mystical Body of Christ is observed in its fullest meaning. Through uncompromising love, little Audrey Santo, as helpless as can be to society, is as helpful as can be to God and her fellow man.

Audrey is one life, helping perhaps hundreds of lives and even thousands of souls. She is the ultimate example of Scripture's words, seemingly last among us but first in the eyes of God. Her life is a living, breathing testimony to the life of Christ and to all other innocent victims. Her mission is the mission of every member of the Body of Christ, no greater or lesser. Once again, all this can be summed up in one word-*love*!

Moreover, little Audrey's life calls us to meditate upon the mystery of love. Her life is love, sacrificed to love. As she did with her own family, Audrey calls us to offer ourselves in the service of love and in honor of love. Her life is to have love burn deeply into our hearts, minds, bodies and souls.

In the end, through her own life, Audrey tells us about our own lives. It is what Scripture tells us about St. John the Apostle. And when he was an old man and unable to preach any more, St. John supposedly told those whom he met only to love. He repeated this so often that someone reportedly said to him, "Why do you always ask people to love?" He replied, *"Because the Master said so."*

Through Audrey's life all souls can witness the Way, the Truth and Life that Christ promised. She teaches us that to truly live and love in Christ, we must live and love like Christ. Thus, we are confronted with the Master's words, **"What you do to the least, you do to Me."**

Ironically, these words again present a formula for peace in our world. For if every person faced this truth, if individuals started caring for one another, and stopped hurting or disdaining their fellow brother or sister, then peace would surely spread throughout the world.

This is perhaps the real miracle of Audrey's life. For in her family's response to her, in their heroic sacrifice and unselfish love, a wonderful example of Scripture's call has been presented to the world. And this incentive serves as an example of how we can work to end the "Culture of Death" and to bring the "Era of Peace".

Indeed, the entire Santo family are suffering servants. And like Audrey, their suffering is innocent, yet offered in a loving way, for the Santo family has responded in union with Christ. And it is precisely when love is difficult that it is most effective in bringing the power of Christ into the world to save.

Therefore, under normal circumstances, people would perhaps look at Audrey and say how terrible it is. But instead, when they come in contact with Audrey, Linda and the entire Santo family, and all the love, instead of saying how terrible it is, they say how wonderful – how wonderful to be around so much love!

PRAY FOR ME, LITTLE AUDREY

From Omaha, Nebraska; from Baltimore, Maryland; from Scottsdale, Arizona; from Ontario, Canada; and from Italy, Poland, South America and Australia, once a year people from all over the world converge upon Worcester, Massachusetts. They come to celebrate. And they come to remember and to thank God for a little girl who has made their lives fuller and richer in one way or another.

Each year on the anniversary of Audrey's accident, August 9th, six to eight hundred people along with up to three dozen priests, pack into Christ the King Church in Worcester for a commemorative Mass, the Divine Mercy Chaplet, and the Rosary. It is a powerful, engaging show of unity that is centered on God's love for and through a little girl that everyone present believes has been "chosen".

While the reality of Audrey's physical state hangs over the assembly like a cloud that will not dissipate, the mystery of how God is using her fills the air. The assembled family, friends and participants believe that they are all part of something so special, so unique and so divine, that only joy, hope, love and faith can come from their gathering. Indeed, it is a celebration of life. God has proven once again through the life of Audrey Santo that good can arise from sadness and despair, tragedy and pain. It is the age-old adage repeatedly proven to be true: No matter what, God can take anything bad and turn it into good – if we let Him.

Certainly with Audrey Santo, an entirely new plane of reality surrounds this truth. God has not only brought about good, but He has also parted the Heavens in a special way. Indeed, the supernatural character of what is transpiring around Audrey has all but revealed the very face of God to our present generation. For God has moved mightily for reasons known only to Him, showering His people with an outpouring of graces in order to bring them love and healing.

Thus, it is no surprise how the events surrounding the life of little Audrey parallel many of the events that surrounded the life of Christ Himself. Audrey Santo, in her innocence, in her tragic, suffering life, and in the healing and hope she brings to so many, walks the same path that our dear Savior trod. And although we remain mystified by much of it, Audrey's apparent state of suffering in Christ as a sinless, innocent victim continues a mystery that cuts to the core of the Christian message to the world. This message proclaims: God so loved His people that He became incarnate as a man in order to die on the cross for their eternal salvation.

Over the centuries, through souls like little Audrey Santo, each generation has been offered this truth in a different way. Audrey's life in Christ is presented as a gift for our salvation. It is a gift of faith that even allows us to go beyond faith, for to deny what we see and hear surrounding her life would be truly obstinate.

Most of all, what we see and hear through Audrey is the message of the Church: the call to the Eucharist and to the message of the Gospel. Nothing is in error here; both are calls to healing, unity and peace through Jesus Christ.

Those experts who have studied the events surrounding Audrey's mission especially point to the four Eucharistic hosts that appear to have physically changed into the Body and Blood of Christ. For truly, it is in the Eucharist that the mystery of God's great love for His people is forever renewed and revealed. Certainly then, these events must be intended to bring God closer to us.

Indeed, the faithful are called to eat the Body and drink the Blood of the Savior. This is the ultimate sign of unity, and it is what every generation of Christians has held as their most sacred belief. From the catacombs of Rome to the concentration camps of World War II, participants in the Sacrament of Love demonstrate that Christians are one body in Christ, and are willing to suffer and die for this truth. Thus, the gathering at Christ the King Church each year further confirms this reality, as the Eucharist is indeed the high point of the celebration that day.

Likewise, the annual gathering at Christ the King Church goes to the heart of the Gospel's message: Salvation begins and ends for each person according to their own response in faith.

As we walk the path of life, every God-fearing soul is called to make an active decision to reject sin and to live life according to the Gospel. With this decision, every possibility and hope for good in a person's life is advanced, for Christ's life and words then become the center of that life. Hence, all actions in a person's life now stem from that center, leading to their eternal reward.

According to Scripture, each person then also shines forth as a beacon, reflecting the Lord's light upon on all whom he meets. Each soul becomes a source of hope, love, healing and peace which can then be spread around the world, one soul at a time. This has occurred with Audrey, thus pointing out, as Scripture promises, that from the bad in our lives good can still come.

At Medjugorje, this is also the message Mary has brought from God for our lost generation. Our Lady is telling us that if we turn away from the root of all evil — sin — we will begin to experience healing and peace. It is the peace that God so earnestly wants us to enjoy. It is a peace founded on fidelity and giving of ourselves, and it is strengthened by sacrifice and love.

It is a peace that must begin with the individual and the family, and then through prayer and faith, it can become the cornerstone of society. This then is Our Lady's plan: to create a world filled with peace which has returned to God through the hands of its Mother. This is the call each of us is to accept. Through conversion and by living a life that focuses on the words of the Gospel, each of us can bring peace into the world, just as Mary says.

In today's distressed and sick world, this plan, at its core, is really a plan of healing. The world will only improve if it is healed. It must be healed of the terrible ravages of sin that now cover it like a cancerous growth. Once more, for those who journey to Christ the King Church each year to be with Audrey and her family, the beginning of this "healing of the world" can be found in many of them for they come as living testimonies to this truth.

Some come because they believe that they have already been physically or spiritually healed through Audrey's intercession. Some come hoping to be healed in body or spirit, or both. Yet, many of them come just because of Audrey. They are like her, for they choose to help carry her cross along with their own, in order to bring healing. In essence, these souls come to unite their crosses with Audrey's, in order to bring healing to others, to themselves, to the Church and to the world.

Healing has always been the ultimate sign of the truth of Jesus Christ and Christianity. From the time Christ walked the earth until now, those with faith in Him and His words have experienced healing. No other religion can claim this. In no other name has there been such healing. Indeed, for two thousand years, millions have claimed healing through and in Christ. From the woman who touched Christ's cloak, to the very next miracle the Church will authenticate in order to canonize a saint, Christ died on the cross to heal His people of their diseased souls and bodies and to give them life in Him.

At Christ the King Church each August 9th, these mysteries of the Eucharist, the Gospel, unity and healing in Christ are truly inspiring. It is a powerful sight, as reconciliations and forgiveness abound, and more miracles occur each year. What God is doing through Audrey Santo brings graces for all to see.

Therefore, is little Audrey, the silent, suffering child, a saint in our midst because of all this? Is she, as Fr. Charles Babbit declared, *"a living saint"*?

Surely, Audrey would be the first to say no. And while there are those who may become angry or critical of such talk, this does not erase the reality of the situation. Like Mother Teresa of Calcutta and other great souls throughout Church history, such as St. Anthony and St. Francis who were also being proclaimed saints while still alive, the life and mission of little Audrey Santo exhibits signs that are reminiscent of the lives of the saints.

Once more, it is recalled that Linda always prayed for a saint, and that soon after the accident, a priest told her, *"you have your saint."* But amazingly, an additional sign of forthcoming grace was perhaps allowed on the very day Audrey was born. At that time, another mysterious event occurred, a healing which could be traced directly to Audrey's life.

On December 19, 1983, Audrey Marie Santo was delivered with the umbilical cord wrapped around her neck. Her entire body was black. She was eight weeks premature, and weighed only five pounds and three ounces. But the fact that she was born at all made her a miracle baby, for besides her premature delivery and small size, her mother, Linda, was very sick at the time.

The doctors had diagnosed Linda with cervical, uterine and breast cancer. In fact, they initially believed that Audrey was a "tumor." Additionally, Linda had only one ovary and a collapsed intrauterine tube. The doctors considered Audrey "a high risk" pregnancy.

Near the time of Audrey's birth, the doctors had to remove tissue from the bottom of Linda's feet in order to perform a biopsy. Her feet were excoriated since the doctors needed to see if her cancer had spread. After the procedure, Linda's feet were covered with blisters.

But soon after Audrey's birth, Linda's husband, Stephen, made a startling discovery. Upon entering the recovery room where Linda rested, he noticed that her exposed feet had somehow totally changed.

"It's gone!" Stephen Santo exclaimed upon closer examination of Linda's feet. "It's all gone. The disease is gone. The blisters are gone. Look at your feet!"

Linda picked up her leg to look at the bottom of one foot and then the other, and she couldn't believe her eyes. Her feet were now "baby pink" in color with no trace of the sores that had recently been there.

That's her first miracle," her husband noted in jest. Indeed, the "miracle baby" somehow seemed to be related to a miraculous healing of her own mother. Not long afterward, Linda's cancer was also diagnosed as having mysteriously vanished.

So, from the day of Audrey's birth until the present, the miracle baby continues to bring miracles of unity, healing and love, just as all saints do.

While the great outpouring of love every August 9th at Christ the King Church is special, the rest of the year is not much different. At 64 South Flagg Street, each week the crowds come to visit little Audrey. Dragging their sorrows and illnesses with them, they come to pray and to celebrate Mass in the Santo home's little chapel, which was once the garage. Afterward, the visitors slowly make their way back through the house to Audrey's room, where they then peer into her bedroom through a large window. There, the guests empty their hearts and souls upon a little girl who lays permanently confined, as if stationed to receive whatever souls bring her. Tears flow, while lips silently move in prayer to and for Audrey. Only God knows what each soul feels and experiences. And only God knows what and how Audrey shares in it all. But like the souls who surround God in eternal bliss, He somehow appears to permit His little suffering servant to receive souls' humblest intentions and their heaviest crosses.

Outside, the voices of children Audrey's age ring out as they jump up and down on the neighbors' trampoline. School-age youngsters laugh and converse as they leave the school bus and make their way home from school each day. Audrey's brother and his friends race around the basketball court in front of her room. And inside, Audrey goes about her day, too - obediently and lovingly delivering to the Lord the day's sorrows and hopes which have been deposited at her bedroom door.

Although every prayer may not be answered the way some would like, when people see Audrey, it helps them to accept the pain of their own lives. It helps them to go forward. It helps to remind them of what their Savior told them long ago, that their lives should involve picking up their crosses and following Him. And they can't deny that little Audrey has apparently done just that.

And so Audrey continues her work of love, day after day, week after week, year after year, just as she has done for over nine years. But as the visitors depart each week, as they slowly make their way home after witnessing such a miraculous place, some indeed come to accept Audrey for who she is - the suffering little servant of the Lord. Perhaps some even believe that this is what God had in mind for her when she was born.

But not Audrey's mother. She knows better. Regardless of all that has occurred, regardless of all the miracles, regardless of the thousands who have come, Linda still directs her prayers for one more healing, for one more miracle - that of Audrey's healing. For although Audrey Santo has become a great source of healing for so many, it doesn't mean that Linda Santo will stop pleading with the Lord for Audrey's complete recovery.

"I ask for Audrey's healing every day," said Linda. "It's not something I do as a prayer once in a while. I pray for it all the time. Everything I do I offer for her. I'm her mom, what else would I want. All my waking hours, I say it consistently, *'Come on, God. You do all this. Get her up! Get her up!'*"

Like Our Lady at the foot of the cross, Linda can't help but ask for such a miracle, even though God has taken Audrey's accident and used it for such incredible good. And although so many miracles have occurred, everyone involved with this "chosen child" longs to see her whole again and to witness her "resurrection".

But while Linda prays for her daughter's healing, on August 9, 1996, as eight hundred souls prayed together in Christ the King Church before the four miraculous Hosts, a different miracle of healing and unity perhaps again occurred through Audrey's powerful prayer. One more blessing came from her life of sacrifice.

No, this miracle did not involve Audrey's healing. Rather, it was once again for Linda and for the Santo family. For after eight years of being away from home, Audrey's father, Stephen Santo, returned to Linda, his children and especially to his God.

No one can precisely describe the feelings of those who shared in this happiness for the Santo family, who are now once more together, healed and whole. Likewise, no one can say for sure that such an unexpected event came from this suffering, silent child. But it is certain that God would not begrudge any soul who may be in search of a similar grace or healing in their life.

And so, while Audrey dutifully goes about her mission each day, no one should be afraid to utter the words so many have come to say:

"Pray for me, little Audrey. Pray for me!!!"

Findings of the Diocese of Worcester

Statement by Most Rev. Daniel P. Reilly, Bishop of Worcester

Over the past eleven years, many unexplainable circumstances have occurred around an innocent, bed-ridden girl named Audrey Santo. In cooperation with the family. I have asked a team of esteemed medical and theological professionals to review the situation to determine its possible impact, negative or positive on the family and the Catholic Faithful.

After a year of careful planning and evaluation, the commission has reported its preliminary findings to me. A summary of those findings is available to anyone who requests them, but I want to share some specific thoughts and concerns at this time as Bishop of the Diocese of Worcester.

The most striking evidence of the presence of God in the Santo home is seen in the dedication of the family of Audrey. Their constant respect for her dignity as a child of God is a poignant reminder that God touches our lives through the love and devotion of others.

There are inexplicable manifestations of oils and substances emanating from religious objects in the Santo home. They are still under study. The purpose of the Church's investigation is not simply to become a promoter of claims of the miraculous. Rather, it is to review the theological foundations for such claims to assure that the faithful who follow them are not being misled.

In the case of Audrey herself, more study is needed from medical and other professionals regarding her level of awareness and her ability to communicate with the people around her. This is critical to the basis of the claim of her ability to intercede with God. In the meantime. I urge continued prayers for Audrey and her family. But praying to Audrey is not acceptable in Catholic teaching.

We are not yet able to confirm claims of miraculous events occurring at Audrey's home or as a result of a visit to Audrey, or from the oils associated with her. One need not make a personal visit to the Santo home. Indeed, continued demand for personal visitation poses the risk of compromising the family's ability to continue to offer excellent care to their daughter.

Further study has also been recommended and approved by me regarding the composition and source of the oils and other substances. In doing this, I want to underscore that any paranormal occurrences are not miraculous in and of themselves. The consistent practice of the Catholic Church has been not to use such occurrences as verifications of miraculous claims.

Finally, more systematic study must be done before the Church can even begin to evaluate the concept of "victim soul", which has been applied to Audrey. We must proceed quite cautiously here, since this term is not commonly used by the Church except for Christ himself who became the victim for our sins and transgressions on the cross.

While further study is being conducted, please pray for Audrey, for her family and for all those seeking healing and hope. I also ask for prayers to assist us so that this continued investigation will strengthen our faith in God's divine mercy and love.

Summary Report
Introduction:

The commission named by Bishop Reilly has completed its first phase of investigation of the extraordinary claims resulting from occurrences surrounding Audrey Santo, a young girl who has been in her family's care since an accidental near drowning eleven years ago. After developing a systematic method for investigation, the commission in this phase had as its objective the analysis of existing documents and materials as well as first hand witnessing of some of the "other than normal" experiences which were occurring at the home.

What was the focus of the commission?

The commission was responsible for developing a methodology for investigation consistent with Catholic teaching on these matters. It included the following four areas:

1. Explanation of "paranormal" occurrences in the Santo home, namely the emitting of oils from statues and other religious objects and the presence of red stains which some say look like blood on four consecrated hosts.

2. The ability of Audrey to communicate, at least to recognize the presence of others around her and to comprehend what is being said to her.

3. The response of the family as it deals with this demanding situation regarding their youngest child, the paranormal activities occurring in the house and the requests by increasingly larger numbers of outsiders to visit Audrey.

Specifically, is the family or someone else causing the paranormal activities to occur through some form of chicanery? What is the quality of the family's general care and concern for their daughter? Does the family attempt to exploit interest in their situation for financial gain? Does the family seek notoriety from the situation? Does the family in any way seek to manipulate those who visit in order to direct their interpretation of the situation?

4.   The basis for the theological interpretations surrounding the claims, including: Are there miracles occurring that can be attributed directly to Audrey? Is Audrey capable of being a victim soul, a title attributed to her by some people? Are the claims being made in keeping with Catholic teachings? Are the daily religious rituals and practices being performed according to approved liturgical practice? Are the Catholic faithful at risk from anything when they visit the home or read materials from the Apostolate, which reports on Audrey, or view videotapes about Audrey? Is there the potential of a "cult forming outside the control of the family of the Apostolate? How does the Church explain the appearance of oils, blood, and other paranormal activities?

Although we can't explain why oils and claims of blood are appearing on religious articles in the home, there is no obvious evidence of chicanery. There is the need to have controlled tests performed involving some of the religious articles and lab analysis of resulting oils or other secretions since no two reports from past tests have come back with the same results.

Is the presence of this "mysterious" oil significant?

The presence of oil is not proof, direct or indirect, of the miraculous. Paranormal activities in and of themselves, according to the perspective and practice of the Catholic Church, do not provide a basis for proving the miraculous. This has been the Church's confirmed directive for hundreds of years sine Pope Benedict XIV. (1740-1758)

When one applies fundamental rules of logic to the situation, even if the presence of the oil cannot be explained, one cannot presume that the inability to explain something automatically makes it miraculous. It certainly calls for scientific research and we will continue to do so.

We must be careful not identify this oil as "holy oil", which could be used to anoint a person. The Sacrament of the Anointing of the Sick, which can only be celebrated by a priest or bishop, uses oil blessed by the bishop at the Mass of Chrism, and is given to those who are seriously ill. This oil is properly called "oil of the sick". Additionally, an anointing by a priest or a bishop may be celebrated as part of a Eucharistic Liturgy for those who are ill, using oil blessed following the Rite of Anointing and Pastoral Care of the Sick.

The Church is responsible for determining the essential elements for the celebration of sacraments and how they are to be administered. Church law calls for pure olive oil or other plant oil to be used in the celebration of the sacrament. Consequently, the Church maintains that this "mysterious oil" should not be used in anointing a person who is ill.

Can Audrey communicate?

While family members claim that Audrey is able to communicate, there is no data to corroborate that claim from the available documentation of the medical professionals who have been involved in her care. With the family's cooperation, there is the need to perform specific testing using professionally accepted methods to determine brainwave activity when subjected to various external stimuli, for example the arrival and departure of family members from her room.

How has the family been responding, from the Church's perspective?

The family's constant love and devotion to their daughter is a miracle in the broad sense of the word. They have always recognized the human dignity of their daughter, despite the circumstances. And, they never cease to open up the door to their home as well as their hearts to the needs of the suffering who write to them and call upon them each day.

More than anything else, those who visit the family make note of the excellent care the family gives to their daughter. This has manifested itself in her physical condition, for example, she has not apparently had bedsores in the eleven years she has been confined to her bed.

Does the family seek financial gain from the situation?

There is no evidence that the family has sought financial gain for themselves. On the contrary, they have not sold the oil, which appears in their home and the Apostolate request only nominal donations for videotapes and other materials about Audrey. These donations are used to assist the Apostolate in the costs incurred to correspond with those who have written to Audrey and to publish a periodic newsletter about Audrey.

Notoriety is of some concern. The family does not seek it for themselves but they certainly do so for Audrey. This has led some people to expect intercessions from Audrey and / or miracles long before anyone has had a chance to evaluate these claims more thoroughly. It has also put the family in a more awkward position of having far more demand for personal visits than it can ever accommodate while continuing to offer excellent care for their daughter.

Are visitors manipulated in order to experience certain things?

Staged or planned manipulation of the visitors to the house is not apparent. The general attitude in the house is friendly, warm and inviting without any sanctimony or undue reverence. However, it must be pointed out that the groups arriving together as they do. Often tend to share certain characteristics in facing terminal illness (their own or that of a loved one) or, at least, tend to be far from skeptical regarding the possibility of experiencing a miracle.

Is the Church ready to say one way or another if miracles attributed to Audrey are occurring?

It will take significant time and resources to determine if miracles are directly attributable to Audrey. Many of the cases cited publicly concerning Audrey's intercession have had medical opinions, which did not rule out the potential for normal recovery (in whole or in part.) Before any objective investigation can be done directly on this question, issues such as Audrey's level of consciousness an ability to communicate need to be corroborated (see above request for further testing.) There will also be the need to set up a clearing-house involving medical authorities to review specific claims of physical cures.

Is Audrey a Victim Soul?

The term "victim soul" is not an official term in the Church. It was used in some circles in the 18th and 19th century when there was a fascination with suffering and death, in an attempt to offer the possibility that one person could suffer for another. Christians believe that Jesus is the sacrificial lamb, the victim for our sins. His suffering and death redeemed humanity form sin and eternal death. Through baptism we share in christ's death with the hope that we will share in his resurrection, his glory. To begin to consider this notion of "victim soul" with regards to Audrey, one would have to establish a corroborated understanding of Audrey's cognitive abilities. This has yet to be done. Beyond that, one would have to determine that Audrey, at the age of three was, and presently, is, capable of making a free choice to accept the suffering of others.

Are there practices at the family's house which are contrary to acceptable Catholic rituals?

Fidelity to the sacraments and to approved liturgical rituals has been noted. Specific areas of concern, such that they should be discontinued regardless of the outcome of this investigation, are as follows:

1.   One should only pray <u>for</u> Audrey. Our faith teaches us to pray to God and to pray for the intercession of the saints. Therefore, the distribution of a "Prayer to Audrey" should cease immediately.

2   Whether or not claims of blood are proven to be present on the consecrated Eucharist in the tabernacle in the home, it must be presented in the context that the transubstantiation we witness at every celebration of the Eucharist is the same. There should be no implications that hosts consecrated at Mass in the Santo home are "better" or even unique. When used in Benediction or Exposition, only on consecrated host should be used, in keeping with approved liturgical practice.

Are there any priests officially assigned as chaplains or spiritual directors to Audrey?

No. Priests who are involved with the family are acting on their own behalf in personally working with the family. Audrey and her family are members of Christ the King parish. The pastor of Christ the King if responsive to and available for their spiritual needs.

Is the investigation over?

The first phase of the investigation, which was to compare existing reports for possible corroboration, is complete. Additional quantifiable study is needed, as cited above in this document, in order to attempt to define the composition of the oil and to verify other claims, as well as to determine Audrey's ability to recognize and respond to outside stimuli. Those tests need to be done before determining whether further theological investigation is warranted.

IN GOD'S HANDS

END NOTES

Chapter 1 -
1. John L. Haffert, *Her Own Words to a Nuclear Age* (Asbury, New Jersey: 101 Foundation, Inc., 1993), p. 35.

Chapter 9 -
1. Author's Interview with Joyce O'Neal.
2. Ibid.
3. Ibid.

Chapter 10 -
1. Author's Interview with Joyce O'Neal.
2. Ibid.

Chapter 11 -
1. Author's Interview with Joyce O'Neal.
2. Authorized quote via Santo family.

Chapter 12 -
1. Article by Neal Isakson, *Catholic Free Press*, July 8, 1988.
2. Ibid.

Chapter 14 -
1. Michael Freze. S.F.O. *They Bore the Wounds of Christ -- The Mystery of the Sacred Stigmata* (Huntington, Indiana: Our Sunday Visitor Publishing Division, 1989), pp. 11-12.
2. Ibid.
3. Ibid.
4. Ibid.

Chapter 15 -
1. Rev. Albert J. Hebert, S.M. *Signs Wonders and Response*

(Paulina, Lousisiana, Hebert, 1988), p. VI.

2. Ibid., p. VIII.

3. Authorized quote via Santo Family.

Chapter 16 -

1 .—., *Audrey's Life - Voice of a Silent Soul* (Video), (St. Louis Missouri: The Mercy Foundation, 1996).

2. Hebert, Op Cit., 1988, p. 62.

3. Don Stefano Gobbi, *Our Lady Speaks to Her Beloved Priests* (St. Francis, Maine: National Headquarters of the Marian Movement of Priests in the United States of America, 1988), p. 107.

Chapter 17 -

1. Letter to Fr. Sylvester Catallo from Joanne Erickson, used with permission of the Santo family.

2.—. *Audrey's Life - Voice of a Silent Soul* (Video), Op. Cit.

3. Report of Abbe Laurentin used with permission of the Santo family.

Chapter 18 -

1. —, *The New American Bible* (Witchita, Kansas: Catholic Bible Publishers, 1984-85 Edition).

2. Ibid.

3. Ibid.

4. Ibid.

5. Ibid.

6. Ibid.

7. Ibid.

8. Ibid.

9. Ibid.

10. Ibid.

Chapter 19 -

1. —., *Audrey's Life - Voice of a Silent Soul* (Video), Op. Cit.

2. —., *The New American Bible*. Op. Cit.

3. —., *Audrey's Life - Voice of a Silent Soul* (Video), Op. Cit.

4. Thomas W. Petrisko, (editor) *Our Lady Queen of Peace, Special Edition I* (Pittsburgh, Pennsylvania: Pittsburgh Center for Peace, Inc., 1995), p. 16.

5. Ibid.

Chapter 20 -

1. Venerable Mary of Agreda, *The Mystical City of God* (Rockford, Illinois: TAN Books and Publishers, Inc., 1978), p. 102.

2. Rev. Eugene M. Brown, *Dreams, Visions & Prophecies of Don Bosco*. (New Rochelle, New York: Don Bosco Publications, 1986), p. 7.

3. Ibid., p. 9.

4. Father Joseph Dirvin, C.M. *Saint Catherine Laboure of Sister Mary of the Holy Trinity* (Rockford, Illinois: TAN Books and Publishers, Inc., 1973), p. 36.

5. Ibid., p. 86.

6. Ibid., p. 86.

7. Ibid., p. 93.

8. Ibid., p. 94.

Chapter 21 -

1. Mary Alice Dennis, *Melanie* (Rockford, Illinois: TAN Books and Publishers, Inc., 1995), p. 3.

2. Ibid.

3. Ibid.

4. Ibid., p. 4.

5. Ibid.

6. Ibid.

7. Saint Therese of Lisieux, *The Story of a Soul*, New York, New York: Image Books, Doubleday, 1989, pp. 66-67.

8. Haffert, Op. Cit., p. 420.

9. Ibid., p. 345.

10. Pope John Paul II, *Crossing the Threshhold of Hope,* (New York, New York, Alfred A. Knopf, 1994), p. 221.

Chapter 22 -
1. Petrisko, Op. Cit. p. 16.
2. Thomas W. Petrisko, *The Last Crusade*, (Pittsburgh, Pennsylvania: St. Andrew's Productions. 1996), p. 39.
3. Michael H. Brown, *The Final Hour* (Milford, Ohio: Faith Publishing Company, 1994), p. 245.
4. ----., *Audrey's Life - Voice of a Silent Soul* (Video), Op. Cit.

Chapter 24
1. Rev. George W. Kosicki, *Intercession* (Milford, Ohio: Faith Publishing Company, 1996), p. X.
2. Ibid. p. 1.
3. Ibid., p. 3.
4. Report from Skin Pathological Laboratory used with permission of Santo Family.

Chapter 25
1. H.S. Research Laboratory, used with permission of Santo family.
2. ----. *Audrey's Life - Voice of a Silent Soul* (Video), Op. Cit.
3. Ibid.
4. Author's interview with John Clote.

Chapter 26
1. Pope John Paul II, Op. Cit., p. 221.
2. Author's interview with John Clote.

Note: All quoted material from the Santo family, their medical staff, Fr. Emmanuel McCarthy, Fr. Joyce, John Clote, Fr. Meade and Judge Dan Lynch were taken from author's personal interviews unless otherwise designated.

IN GOD'S HANDS

SELECTED BIBLIOGRAPHY

Agreda, Venerable Mary of. *The Mystical City of God*. Rockford, Illinois: TAN Books and Publishers, Inc., 1978.

----. *Audrey's Life - Voice of a Silent Soul* (Video), St. Louis Missouri: The Mercy Foundation, 1996.

Ball, Ann. *Modern Saints*. Rockford, Illinois: TAN Books and Publishers, Inc., 1983.

Bartulica, Nicholas, M.D. *Medjugorje: Are the Seers Telling the Truth?* Chicago, Illinois: Croatian Franciscan Press, 1991.

Borelli, Antonio A. & John R. Spann. *Our Lady of Fatima: Prophecies of Tragedy on Hope for America and the World*. United States: The American Society for the Defense of Tradition, Family and Property, 1985.

Brown. Rev. Eugene M. *Dreams, Visions & Prophecies of Don Bosco*. New Rochelle, New York: Don Bosco Publications, 1986.

Brown, Michael H. *The Final Hour*. Milford, Ohio: Faith Publishing Company, 1992.

Butler, Fr. Alban. *Lives of the Saints*. Rockford, Illinois: TAN Books and Publishers, Inc., 1995.

Carty, Rev. Charles Mortimer. *Padre Pio The Stigmatist*. Rockford, Illinois: TAN Books and Publishers, Inc., 1973.

Craig, Mary. *The Mystery of the Madonna of Mejugorje Spark from Heaven*. Notre Dame, Indiana: Ave Maria Press, 1988.

Cruz, Joan Carroll. *Secular Saints*. Rockford, Illinois: TAN Books and Publishers, Inc., 1989.

Dennis, Mary Alice. *Melanie*. Rockford, Illinois: TAN Books and Publishers, Inc., 1995.

Dirvin, Father Joseph, C.M. *Saint Catherine Laboure of Sister Mary of the Holy Trinity*. Rockford, Illinois: TAN Books and Publishers, Inc., 1987.

Duboin, Rev. Alain-Marie, O.F.M. *The Life and Message of Sister Mary of the Holy Trinity*. Rockford, Illinois: TAN Books and Publishers, Inc., 1987.

----. *Exploring Fatima*. Washington, New Jersey: AMI Press, 1989.

Freze, Father Michael, S.F.O. *The Making of Saints*. Huntington, Indiana: Our Sunday Visitor, Inc., 1991.

Freze, Father Michael, S.F.O. *They Bore the Wounds of Christ -- The Mystery of the Sacred Stigmata*. Huntington, Indiana: Our Sunday Visitor Publishing Division, 1989.

Haffert, John M. *Her Own Words to a Nuclear Age*. Asbury, New Jersey: 101 Foundation, Inc., 1993.

Haffert, John M. *You, Too!* Asbury, New Jersey: Lay Apostolate Foundation, 1995.

Hebert, Rev. Albert J., S.M. *The Discernment of Visionaries and Apparitions Today*. Paulina, Louisiana: Hebert, 1994.

Hebert, Rev. Albert J., S.M. *Signs Wonders and Response*. Paulina, Louisiana: Hebert, 1988.

----. *Inchigeela A Call to Prayer*. Ireland: Inchigeela Queen of Peace Group, 1989.

----. John Paul II, Pope. *Crossing the Threshold of Hope*. New York: Alfred A. Knopf, 1994.

Johnston, Francis. *Alexandrena The Agony and The Glory*. Rockford, Illinois: TAN Books and Publishers, Inc., 1979

Kosicki, Rev. George W. C.S.B. *Intercession*. Milford, Ohio: Faith Publishing Company, 1996.

Laffineur, Fr. Matiene and M.T. le Pelletier. *Star on the Mountain*. Lindenhurst, New York: Our Lady of Mount Carmel de Garabandal, Inc., 1969.

Laurentin, Fr. Rene and Ljudevit Rupcic. *Is the Virgin Mary Appearing at Medjugorje?* Washington, D.C.: The Word Among Us Press, 1984.

----. *Little Nellie of Holy God* (pamphlet). Long Beach California: Litho Tech Impressions, 1993.

Lynch Daniel J. *Our Lady of Guadalupe and Her Missionary Image*. St. Albans, Vermont: The Missionary Iage of Our Lady of Guadalupe, Inc., 1993.

Mariamante. *The Apostolate of Holy Motherhood*. Milford, Ohio: The Riehle Foundation, 1991.

----. *Marthe Robin*. (pamphlet - no publisher or date given).

McCarthy, Reverend Charles, *The Stigmata & Modern Science*, Rockford, Illinois, Tan Books and Publisher, Inc., 1974.

Miravalle, Mark, S.T.D. *Heart of the Message of Medjugorje*. Steubenville, Ohio: Franciscan University Press, 1988.

----. *New American Bible*. (St. Joseph Meduim Size Edition) New York, New York: Catholic Book Publishing Co., 1991.

Odell, Catherine M. *Those Who Saw Her The Apparitions of Mary*. Huntington, Indiana: Our Sunday Visitor, Inc., 1986.

Petrisko, Thomas W. *Call of the Ages*. Santa Barbara, California: Queenship Publishing Company, 1995.

Petrisko, Thomas W. *For the Soul of the Family*. Santa Barbara, California: Queenship Publishing Company, 1996.

Petrisko, Thomas W. *The Last Crusade*. McKees Rocks, Pennsylvania: St. Andrew's Productions, 1996.

Petrisko, Thomas W. *The Sorrow, the Sacrifice, and the Triumph, The Apparitions, Visions and Prophecies of Christina Gallagher*. New York: Simon and Schuster, Inc. 1995.

Peyret, Rev. Raymond. *Marthe Robin The Cross and the Joy*. staten Island New York: Alba House, 1981.

Rengers, Christopher, OFM Cap. *The Youngest Prophet*. Staten Island, New York: Alba House - Society of St. Paul, 1986.

Robin, Marthe. *The Cross and the Joy*. Staten Island, New York: Alba House, 1981.

Rufin, Bernard. *Padre Pio: The True Story*. Huntington, Indiana: Our Sunday visitor Publishing Division, 1991.

Tanquerey, Adolphe, S.S.D.D. *The Spiritual Life -- A Treatise on*

Ascetical and Mystical Theology. Westminster, Maryland: The Newman Pres.

----. *The Holy Bible Douay Rheims Version.* Rockford, Illinois: TAN Books and Publishers, Inc.

----. *The New American Bible.* Witchita, Kansas: Catholic Bible Publishers, 1984-95 Edition.

Thomas, Clayton L. M.D. M.P.H. (ed.) *Taber's Cyclopedic Medical Dictionary.* Philadelphia, Pennsylvania: F.A. Davis Company, 1985.

Trochu, Abbe Francois. *Saint Bernadette Soubirous.* Rockford, Illinois: TAN Books and Publishers, Inc. 1985.

Liseux, Saint Therese of. *The Autobiography of Saint Therese of Liseux.* New York: Image Books - Doubleday, 1989.

Underhill. *Mysticism.* New York: Meridian-New American Library, 1974.

Valtorta, Maria. *The Victim-Souls.* Switzerland: In Wahrheit En Treue, 1991.

Vincent, R. *Please Come Back to Me and My Son.* Milford County, Armaugh, Ireland: Milford House, 1992.

Werfel, Franz. *The Song of Bernadette.* New York: Phoenix Press-Walker and Company, 1988.

----. *What Happened at Pontmain.* Washington, New Jersey: Ave Maria Institute (no date).

----. *Wondrous News From Litmanova.* (Pamphlet - no date or publisher listed)

222

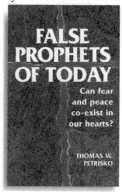

224

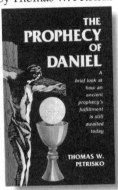

228

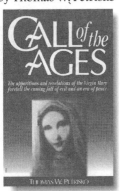

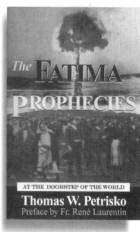

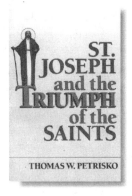

232

About the Cover

After a pilgrimage to Medjugorje, cover artist and designer, Gerry Simboli, found that most of the assignments coming her way were of a spiritual nature. She has designed and illustrated video jackets for "Marian Apparitions of the 20th Century", "The Father's Gift" and a new video about the effects of abortion called "Don't Cry Mary", "The Bridge to Heaven" book jacket is also her work.

Gerry and husband, Joe, a talented designer and woodworker, have created sculpted religious works in wood. One of their creations is the Mother of the Holy Eucharist monstrance where the Mother of God, with humility and in shadow, holds the luna containing the Blessed Sacrament over her heart.

For information about this monstrance, you may write to:

Simboli Design
Box 26
Cheyney, PA 19319
(610) 399-0156